KU-190-453

Reading development and extension

Reading development and extension

Christopher Walker
Senior Lecturer in Education and Reading Tutor
Mather College of Education

Ward Lock Educational

ISBN 0 7062 33638 casebound
0 7062 33646 paperback

First published 1974
Reprinted 1974

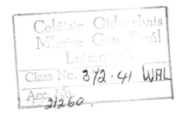

Printed by
Hollen Street Press Limited, Slough
for Ward Lock Educational
116 Baker Street, London W1M 2BB
Made in England

Contents

Part 1

Clearing the ground

Introduction
It seems almost impertinent to write yet another book on the teaching of reading. However, a survey of the literature reveals, despite its enormous volume, that beginning and remedial reading have the major share and that very little has been done about extending the child who comes into the junior school able to read. The infant teachers the child has just left are satisfied that one of their major aims for the child has been achieved – they have started him reading. The junior teachers to whom he comes are probably unable to express with equal clarity what their aims for the child are. If pressed they might suggest that they hope to broaden the child's experience and to develop new skills and interests through the more varied curriculum of the junior school and that they would rely heavily on the child's ability to read to achieve this development. As for reading itself, it would be developed incidentally, through English and the content areas, and by the opportunities provided for writing of many different kinds. The problem here is the word 'incidentally'. If it is thus that reading is to develop, how can the teacher be certain that the different stages and the skills essential at those stages have adequate treatment, that sufficient practice and reinforcement are provided at those stages, and that the most appropriate materials and methods at the different stages are applied? An infant teacher asked such questions would probably give a clear-cut set of responses indicating that she knows where she is going and what she will do on the way. Prereading activities indicate when a formal beginning can be made in earnest. This will involve the use of a reading scheme, usually employing look and say methods, to build up a sight vocabulary and the confidence which accompanies it. At a suitable stage phonics will be introduced and word attack skills taught to complement a constantly increasing sight vocabulary as progress is made through the reading scheme. The skills are reinforced by writing and other teacher-directed activities. At some time towards the end of the infant school period the child will be sufficiently independent in reading to enjoy a wide variety of simple books. It is doubtful if many teachers working beyond the infant stage could summarize with equal cer-

tainty and succinctness a reading methodology for the particular range of children they teach.

The fact is that a well-defined set of reading aims and a methodology for achieving them at levels beyond the beginning stage do not as yet exist in any generally recognizable pattern. The reasons for this are largely historical and stem from the fact that for too long 'reading' has been synonymous with 'beginning reading' which has been the almost exclusive province of the infant teacher. Teacher-training courses have reflected and perpetuated this narrow view of reading. Consequently, the only personnel with any substantial training in teaching reading have been infant teachers, whose courses have not unnaturally concentrated on the beginning stage. Junior teachers have tended to get very little on the teaching of reading and secondary teachers almost nothing at all. Where anything has been done for these two student categories it has generally been at remedial level, i.e. beginning reading for older children.

The influence of training is reflected in the attitude of practising teachers towards reading. Infant teachers regard it as their particular job to get the children started. In general, according to the Kent survey (Morris 1966), they do this with a 75 per cent success rate. Where training courses exist for junior teachers the emphasis is largely on getting the 25 per cent who have still not acquired basic competence through the beginning stage. As a proportion of the slow starters will have achieved mastery at some time during the junior school period, the middle and secondary school teacher is left with only a small minority of children who still find reading difficult. College courses which deal almost exclusively with remedial work, i.e. for a minority of children, will hardly motivate the majority of junior and secondary teachers who are aware that for upwards of 75 per cent of their pupils basic reading poses no severe problems. Their problem is how to extend the majority of children who are already readers. Training courses for teachers of postinfant children should concentrate more on an understanding of the processes involved in the acquisition of the intermediate and higher order skills. From such understanding it should be possible to draw up a set of goals relevant to the needs of postinfant children, a set of teaching techniques and apparatus for achieving them, and an organizational framework which guarantees the time and optimal conditions for goal accomplishment. Aims, methods and organization are the substance of this book. However, to ensure that a reading methodology for the postinfant schools gets off to a good start, it is essential for the junior school to rid itself of the burden of beginning reading at an early stage. Only when this is done will it be possible to concentrate on the major task of reading extension and development. It is useless for teachers of juniors and older children to bemoan the fact that pupils arrive from infant schools unable to read competently. The fact is that children do arrive with this handicap. Junior schools should accept this as one of the facts of life and set about improving matters with some urgency. Morris recommends that as about 25 per cent of children entering junior school need a continuation of the sort of teaching associated with the infant school, first junior classes should be staffed by personnel with infant training or experience. In order to give subsequent classes a good start with more advanced work in reading, the teaching of reading in the first junior year should have priority over all other curriculum subjects. Children with reading difficulties should be identified early and given regular, systematic attention, fortified by favourable provision of books, materials and resources generally. The longer reading problems persist the harder they are to overcome. However, if a really intensive all-out attack on reading is made in the first junior year, the numbers coming through to subsequent classes still at the beginning stage should be sufficiently small to enable class teachers to cope with them as a minority group, while concentrating on their major task of extending the majority. The rest of this book is largely concerned with that task.

Chapter 1

Aims and attitudes in reading extension

Starting points

Before the teacher can decide what to aim at, it is important for her to know where she is starting from. It was suggested in the introduction that basic competence at the beginning stage is essential before advanced skill teaching is possible, and that the acquisition of the basic skills should be achieved during the first junior year. What is basic competence? How will the teacher at the end of the first, or the beginning of the second, junior year assess the child's readiness for reading treatment of a more advanced kind? The following criteria are suggested:

1 The child has successfully completed a typical infant reading scheme and has read a selection of supplementary readers on the way.
2 He has a minimum reading age of nine years.
3 He has demonstrated an ability to read simple material more rapidly silently than orally.
4 He has developed sufficient powers of concentration to read a story through at one sitting with obvious pleasure and with no apparent signs of finding the experience in any way irksome.

Translating these points into reading terms, the child has sufficient word attack, recognition and organizational skills to operate at a level of literal comprehension with simple materials – he understands the meaning of words, ideas and sentences in context. To do this he must be capable of finding the main idea, outlining the development of the reading matter, summarizing it in his own words and understanding standard syntactical forms.

Reading development is hierarchial in structure. The base has already been described and it is on this base of fundamental skills and abilities that the superstructure of more advanced programmes in reading instruction is built. The apex is the ability to read critically, efficiently and habitually. To fill in the parts in between requires a knowledge of a complex spiral of interrelated factors and a view of reading which sees it as more closely related to thinking than to any other aspect of behaviour.

Critical reading

Helen Robinson (1964) distinguishes twelve abilities, beyond the beginning stage described above, essential to critical reading. These are:

1   recognizing and discriminating between judgments, facts, opinions and inferences
2   comprehending implied ideas
3   interpreting figurative and other nonliteral language
4   detecting propaganda
5   forming and reacting to sensory images
6   anticipating outcomes
7   generalizing within the limits of justifiable evidence
8   making logical judgments and drawing conclusions
9   comparing and contrasting ideas
10 perceiving relationships – of time, space, sequence and cause and effect
11 identifying the author's bias or point of view
12 recognizing and reacting to exceptional diction – satire, irony, cynicism.

Russell (1964) maintains that critical reading is the application of critical thinking to the reading process. He defines critical thinking as a three-factor ability which includes:

1   an attitude factor of questioning and suspended judgment
2   a functional factor which involves the use of methods of logical inquiry and problem-solving
3   a judgment factor of evaluating in terms of some norm or standard or consensus.

If the above analyses are accepted as relevant to our knowledge of what is involved in critical reading, it is important to devise techniques which will ensure that the twelve sets of abilities identified by Robinson and the three stages of thinking postulated by Russell come within the reading experience of the children. Here the question of teacher attitude is especially important for achieving aims. Some teachers might seek to break down critical reading into its separate components and teach each separate aspect systematically. One can envisage separate lessons or series of lessons during which irony, cynicism and satire are distinguished and practice at recognition of these factors is given. One can imagine a unit on detecting propaganda and reading varied examples of it. The list could go on – a session on anticipation, one on the figures of speech, on sensory imagery etc. There are possibly teachers who would not be deterred by the difficulties of breaking down Russell's three factors into their separate elements and giving children graded practice in inferring, judging and the like. However, to compartmentalize the processes of reading in such a way is to be ignorant of the essential nature of reading itself, of the spiral interrelatedness of the many factors which together make reading the type of behaviour that it is. Reading is a synthesis of many skills operating simultaneously and no amount of analysis will make the bits and pieces which result into ongoing reading behaviour. Teachers need to be aware of the general factors and attitudes involved in critical reading and provide the conditions and techniques which will best promote it. Readers can be either passive or active. The passive reader will absorb the printed word without question. The active reader weighs up the pros and cons of what is said, reserving judgment until he has amassed sufficient evidence from the text and related it to his own experience to be able to judge the truth and worth of what the author has said.

The teacher's main aim in producing critical readers is to encourage on the part of his pupils attitudes towards reading which show them as active, questioning, and concerned to resort to textual evidence before giving a point of view.

Efficient reading

Efficient reading may be defined as the ability to read with maximum comprehension in the minimum possible time consistent with the reader's purposes. The most important element in this definition is the reader's purpose, which will determine how well and how quickly reading will be done. If the subject matter is difficult or of crucial importance to the reader, for example when preparing for an examination, speed will be a secondary factor. Rereading, annotation, consultation of other texts may all be necessary to get the full gist of the reading matter. On the other hand, where vocabulary and subject matter are familiar or relatively simple, one can go at a much faster rate without neglecting comprehension. The efficient reader is one who consciously adapts his reading rate to suit his purposes and the difficulty of the material. Unfortunately, the majority of untrained readers do not so adjust. They have one speed and use it for all reading matter regardless of their purposes and the nature of the content. This is patently inefficient. There is a great deal of routine, comparatively trivial reading matter which constantly comes our way in a modern society. This should be dealt with quickly and got out of the way in order to leave time for material which is important. Of course, if important reading matter too can be got through more quickly while maintaining a high level of comprehension, this is a gain in efficiency, giving time either to read more or to spend in other important activities, or simply in increased leisure.

I am constantly surprised when running advanced reading courses (e.g. for staffs of colleges of education) at the grossly inefficient reading habits of very highly educated people. In one such course there were a liberal sprinkling of members of the English department, all with a minimum of a good English honours degree, and several with higher degrees besides. Despite the unquestioned breadth of their reading, they had volunteered to join the course because they felt they were slow readers. At the last minute a young mathematics lecturer, a nongraduate, begged to join the course. He felt guilty that he did not spend as much time reading as he should. Very early in the course it became apparent that the young mathematician was, in fact, a most accomplished reader and at the very beginning was already reading twice as quickly as the best of the English graduates and with equal comprehension. The recognition of his prowess gave his confidence a useful boost and he went on rapidly to double a reading rate that was already well above average and to make significant gains in comprehension.

Now if very highly educated people who have spent some twenty years in full-time education, largely centred on books, still regard themselves (and rightly so) as incompetent readers, how inefficient as readers must be the majority of people who embark on adult life after only ten years of schooling. All children at school could obviously benefit from techniques which would increase their reading rate and powers of comprehension and, more important, enable them to adjust their rates according to their purposes and the nature of the material. Measures to achieve these goals should figure prominently in teachers' aims in reading extension, as should the development of certain locating skills which enable readers to find important sources of information quickly and economically.

Fostering the habit of reading
One of the most significant areas of teacher failure is that though the majority of children can read, they do not in the opinion of their teachers read anything like enough. They can read, but don't. One possible reason for this is the inefficient reading habits already referred to. If a child has only one reading speed and that speed is slow, reading is a chore which does not warrant the considerable time spent on it. One certain reason why children who can read hardly ever do is the competition from other forms of entertainment, notably television. It may be that teachers will have to make some sort of compromise between reading for entertainment and other forms of amusement and admit that children have more accessible and more

numerous activities available than when we ourselves were very young: in short, that reading for pleasure no longer has the importance that it once had. If this is the case, teachers must be clear about what kind of reading is important and make sure that at least is done well.

In my experience not enough incentive to read for sheer pleasure is given in schools beyond the infant stage. Reading is done largely for information, to be regurgitated in topics and project work. It is used as the starting point for writing and other forms of activity which at their best may be described as creative but which are commonly repetitive and unoriginal. Worse, the time occupied by activity of this kind leaves little time for reading for pleasure. Even when children do demonstrate a desire to read for pleasure or to widen long-standing interests or to develop new ones, teachers are frequently ill-equipped to discuss, advise or suggest – all the things essential to stimulate 'the reading bug'. Generally, they cannot organize to have time to do any of these important things. Worse, they do not have the expertise to stretch and inspire the developing reader. They must aim to acquire such expertise as well as make sure that they have time and opportunity to put that knowledge to effect. It is a most important aim to ensure not only that children can read, but do read, and for many purposes, not least among them enjoyment.

Attitude change essential
The aims of developing critical and efficient readers who have a habit and love of reading will not be accomplished without considerable changes of attitude, not only on the part of teachers of junior, middle and secondary schoolchildren, but also on the part of those responsible for training them. Change of attitude in turn depends on a certain willingness to initiate organizational changes. Probably the change likely to make the widest and most immediate impact is in the training field. The illusion that the teaching of reading is the concern solely of the infant school should be dispelled, and in a most positive way, by ensuring that teachers of postinfant children have a longer and more thorough training in the teaching of reading than infant teachers. This is necessary to ensure that children with special difficulties do acquire the basic skills when their particular maturational status makes this possible. In addition, postinfant teachers need relevant courses in higher order skill teaching. Thus junior and secondary teachers would be seen to be more highly qualified in the teaching of reading than infant teachers – they would know all that infant teachers know about the subject and much more besides.

Certain organizational changes in schools are also necessary. In a typical infant school it is obvious that a considerable part of the ongoing activity is devoted to teaching reading. Time, space, staff and materials are allocated and organized for this specific purpose. It is essential to give reading in postinfant schools the sort of status which it obviously has at the infant stage. Here, the most basic of all school subjects, it is regarded as a subject in its own right. It needs to be so regarded in junior, middle and secondary schools. It needs to have a favoured position in the timetable and to be taught regularly and systematically in periods specifically allocated for that purpose, in addition to the sort of incidental treatment which is all that it generally receives at the present time.

Most important of all (and training should have a most positive influence in this respect) teachers of older children should themselves be so equipped for their job that their attitude, if expressed, should unequivocally proclaim 'It's fun to teach reading!' In most schools beyond the infant stage attitudes towards the teaching of reading are quite the reverse of this. Inadequately trained, those junior and secondary teachers who manage in time to acquire some expertise in teaching reading do so by trial and error. This can be a long and painful process, both for the teacher and for the children at whose expense the expertise is acquired. It is unfortunately true that teachers do not teach well subjects of which they are unsure or which they positively dislike. The majority of junior and secondary teachers are unsure about teaching reading and, lacking confidence, rarely approach it with enjoyment. It was not always thus. Inglis (1968) recalls a time when tutors found it difficult 'to coax students away from the reading lesson when it depended on oral recitation from the book, followed by a quiz time known as intelligence'. Despite the current disrepute into which this so-called method has fallen 'it had a value in offering to the teacher and to the pupils an opportunity to discuss many topics in a casual and informative way'. Finally, Inglis recalls that 'teachers felt at home with reading lessons conducted after that fashion and often approached them with a contagious enjoyment'. It should be not the least of our aims to teach reading with enjoyment and to adopt those techniques and forms of organization which will best contribute to that end.

Summary
The aims of teaching reading beyond the beginning stage are to develop readers who are both critical and efficient, who love reading and have formed the habit of reading both for information and for pleasure. To accomplish these aims certain changes of attitude are necessary on the part of teachers and of those who train them. Junior and secondary teachers should have longer and more relevant training in teaching reading than those concerned merely with the beginning stage. In junior, middle and secondary schools reading should have the same sort of status which it enjoys at the infant stage. Incidental teaching should continue but additionally reading must be taught as a

subject in its own right, regularly and systematically. For this purpose, blocks of time must be specifically allocated in the timetable. Reading will not prosper unless it is taught with confidence and enjoyment. Techniques and forms of organization which will contribute to that end must become part of the professional equipment of all who teach subjects requiring their pupils to read.

Chapter 2

Towards a methodology for reading extension

Review of surviving archaic methods
A definite methodological pattern for teaching beginning reading has been established in the infant school. No generally recognizable pattern has as yet emerged at the junior and subsequent levels of schooling. However, isolated examples of archaic practices still survive and it is essential to eradicate these in order to establish a methodology based on sound pedagogical principles and directed towards the achievement of the three main aims described in Chapter 1. The so-called methods referred to are:

1 whole class oral reading
2 group oral reading
3 hearing children reading individually.

The class oral method
This is a survival of the days of payment by results when the basic primer was learned by rote and involves no more than each pupil in the class reading orally in turn from the same basic text. There can be no justification for such a practice today; in fact, it offends good practice on four counts.

First, it disregards the wide spread of individual differences in ability which in the average mixed-ability class produce a range of up to nine years of reading age. One child may be little more than a nonreader. Another in the same class may be a most accomplished reader. In between these two extremes the rest of the class will be spread from poor to good, with a fairly large cluster about the average. Yet despite these obvious differences in ability, all are expected to read the same material.

Second, it ignores individual interests and preferences. Regardless of personal tastes the same matter must be read by all. Such disregard for individual differences in both ability and interests results in boredom for the better readers and frustration and failure for the poorer ones.

B

Third, the accent is on oral reading and hence expression and enunciation tend to have the major emphasis rather than comprehension. The latter is bound to suffer in such an exercise as the pupils can only understand a sentence when they have read it. The way to overcome this difficulty is to give the children opportunities to prepare the reading beforehand, but this is rarely done and who reads what is decided in the most arbitrary manner and not as a result of careful preparation. In fact, changes of reader are dictated by disciplinary needs rather than by the nature of the material, those who are suspected of 'not following' being the most likely candidates to have the distinction of 'being next'.

Fourth, the natural pace and development of the story is constantly broken up by the frequent changes of reader and by the necessity the teacher may feel from time to time to clear up vocabulary and pronunciation difficulties and to counter the many interruptions by occasionally summarizing the material for the children's benefit.

Group oral method
Recognizing the futility of class oral reading, some teachers break down the class into smaller and more homogeneous groups. Unfortunately the groups are then subjected, albeit on a smaller scale, to many of the difficulties inherent in class oral reading. Worse, several groups operate simultaneously in competition, each with a monitor in charge. The teacher usually creates an additional diversion, either by taking the remedial section himself or by rotating from group to group and temporarily displacing the monitor. Whichever of these roles he opts for, the end result is that he effectively loses control over the responsibility for the reading behaviour of almost the entire class. The monitors are chosen for their reading ability which unfortunately is rarely equated with their ability to maintain discipline within their respective groups. The disciplinary problems likely to arise from group oral monitorial reading sessions make even whole class methods seem more desirable. Here at least the teacher is in charge and has some control over overt, if not reading, behaviour. In any case, the teaching role of the monitor is necessarily limited by his immaturity, inexperience and lack of training and status and could rarely be expected to exceed mere prompting or the giving of a minor cue or whole word. Monitors become rapidly frustrated by the difficulties of their task and as they are perforce chosen from the brighter readers, they are usually intelligent enough to realize that their time is being used to benefit others rather than themselves. Resentment at being 'neglected' easily builds up and is reinforced by parental concern that their offspring are not being sufficiently stretched. Some sensitive teachers attempt to compensate their monitors by taking them

together as a reading group once a week. Unfortunately the monitors themselves are good readers and require treatment of a more stimulating kind than can be satisfied by oral parroting of the round-robin type.

When groups are handled in the ways described above it is obvious that their teachers are ignorant of the principles of effective group work. The purpose of group formation is to assemble a relatively homogeneous section of the class in order to work effectively and with maximum economy of teaching resources under the teacher's direction towards some definite reading goal. The value of the group lies in its possibilities for intelligent discussion and participation and for this purpose it must be large enough to make possible a range of viewpoints yet small enough to keep discussion within reasonable bounds and to allow each member to contribute. Oral reading has a purely functional role in group work as when textual evidence is cited to prove a point. At the extension level the bulk of reading done within the group should properly be silent reading. The most important activity to characterize group work should be thinking.

Hearing children read
This method, hearing children read aloud material which they have prepared beforehand, is more properly associated with beginning reading than with reading extension and stems from the mistaken belief that reading instruction must always be on a one to one basis. It is a most uneconomical practice and assumes that in a class of say forty children, thirty-nine can be gainfully employed while the teacher is occupied with one individual. A most sophisticated set of materials would be needed to satisfy the needs of some forty different children and occupy them purposefully while leaving the teacher free to teach each member of the class in turn individually. In practice, of course, it is usually only the children well below average in reading who are given treatment of this kind. This is a pity for the average and brighter readers could profit from occasional individual attention, albeit of a kind different from that described.

These three 'methods' examined above are survivals from an age when attitudes towards teaching reading were quite different from those appropriate to teaching reading extension today. In every case the emphasis is on oral rather than silent reading, an emphasis more obviously relevant to the beginning stage than to levels beyond that of basic competence. It is doubtful if whole class methods will ever be suitable for reading instruction, except for very occasional usage as when contributions by groups or individuals are shared by classmates. However classes are organized a large proportion of the children will be mere passive recipients, the active role being reserved for the group or individual actually contributing at any one time. Group methods have a great deal to offer, especially if members have maximum opportunities for active participation and the teacher is actively engaged in promoting the work in hand. Group oral reading is not recommended because it fails to provide such opportunities. Individual work is essential if pupils are to develop with appropriate material at their own rate. The aim of individual work is to enable each pupil to go as far and as fast as his interests and capacity will permit. However, teachers will need to be involved in much more than merely hearing children read if skill development is to proceed at the pupils' best rate. Appropriate materials will have to be provided and self-correcting procedures will have to be built-in, as will methods by which pupils record their achievements and assume some responsibility for their own progress.

Current approaches to teaching reading

Topic and project approaches
Though class and group oral reading and the practice of hearing children read individually still persist they are not widespread in junior schools today. Their exponents at least have the virtue of giving some time and attention, however misguided, to the teaching of reading, which is more than can be said for the majority of teachers in postinfant schools where reading is haphazard and incidental without any clearly defined structure or definite teaching policy.

Actually the activity which most characterizes our junior, middle and secondary schools today is writing, an activity to which reading plays very much the second fiddle. From the most minimal of reading activity there stems a considerable volume of time-consuming writing, supported by equally time-consuming activities such as tracing, drawing, crayoning, painting, cutting-out and pasting-in, the whole collectively labelled either 'topic' or 'project work'. On inspection, a great deal of the writing turns out to be mere verbatim transcription of whole passages of printed text. Where a minority of children do use texts intelligently and translate what is relevant into their own terms, the end results are often so voluminous as to defy conscientious attempts at marking. Thus a great deal of children's effort goes uncorrected, unrewarded and – worse – undiscussed with their teachers, so that errors remain undetected and are actually reinforced. Now it is one of the objectives of reading to stimulate and generate a variety of interests and activities. What should not happen, however, is that the resultant activities should so dominate the timetable that no time is available to pursue the major aims of reading development. If the only reading which children do is incidental to topic and project work, the teacher has no control over the haphazard nature of whatever learning may result. The project bandwagon has had a long run and with it the whole syndrome of child-centredness. We British teachers proudly proclaim that we are first teachers of children. What is often forgotten is that as well as teaching children we have to teach them something. We have been so concerned to let children learn, preferably from pursuits associated with their own interests, that we often stand back and leave them to it, forgetting that the job of the teacher is to teach. We should be much more concerned with what it is that children learn and with the quality of their learning, and equally with what exactly it is we are teaching and with the quality of our teaching. Our children will not emerge as critical, efficient and habitual readers if our most valuable teaching resource; time, is dissipated by overindulgence in transcription and supporting activities involving the use of paint, crayons, scissors and Sellotape. Reading too needs time, and it will prosper in proportion to the time spent on its development, but only if that time is used effectively with techniques and resources consistently directed to the achievement of clearly defined objectives.

Formal comprehension exercises
Ours is such a varied educational scene that child-centred schools coexist, often in the same districts, with schools of traditional formality where winds of change have hardly penetrated. In these schools too writing is the predominant activity and reading is merely the excuse for and introductory element in an exercise in nit-picking known as 'comprehension'. Because reading almost invariably precedes the questioning this whole procedure is backward-looking and almost entirely at a literal level. In training readers in higher order skills, reading must be seen as a complex process in which the reader by various cues comes to associate his thinking with that of the author – the 'tuning-in' process – and the sooner this is done the sooner will the reader gain insights into which direction the author is going and what are the likeliest outcomes. From the various clues which reveal the author's personal bias, point of view, or final intent as the plot unfolds, the reader is enabled to adjust his mental set to the possible shifts in the story, questioning the author's credibility and relating incident and characterization to his own experience. On the basis of the evidence accumulated on the way, the reader forms hypotheses which are constantly refined as more clues are gathered and which give him final insight into the author's ultimate intent. Thus reading at this level is forward-looking, anticipatory and predictive, active and questioning, and the attitudes essential to reading of this order are unlikely to be developed by backward-looking procedures where reading is reduced to passivity and mere recall by questions which are asked when all has been revealed.

Provision of class and school libraries
Advocates of the incidental and unstructured approach to reading development will be swift to point out that attention to children's

interests has resulted in a most positive gain in one respect at least – the unprecedented spread of children's libraries, whether class, school or community. Obviously, however, if topic and project work is to proceed, books will have to be provided in class and school libraries. Whether the provision of such facilities of itself stimulates the desire to read is questionable. However much books are used in schools to stimulate written and other supporting activities, the fact remains that if reading for pleasure is to survive it will do so because people have developed a habit of reading and with it a love of reading which endures. It is unfortunate that many children never acquire the reading habit and this can only be considered a significant area of teacher failure. As the development of reading tastes and interests is such an individual matter, teachers have largely been defeated by the time factor. To discuss periodically with each child the state of his reading development and to suggest new avenues for his interests takes a considerable amount of time. Also, hitherto few teachers have found the time to keep abreast of children's literature. Very few have even read all the children's books in their own class library. Hence teachers have been particularly poorly placed to advise children on what is good and where it is available, and what books would usefully supplement or extend a given interest. Obviously what is needed is a much more systematic approach towards fostering the love of reading with the time and techniques to accomplish this built into an organized framework of total reading development.

Promotion of reading efficiency
Very little is currently done to develop children's ability to read better and faster, or to apply effective techniques to study-type materials. Few practising teachers have had any useful training in this area of skill development and hence there is little expertise at this level in the majority of school personnel. Almost the only set of materials designed for work of this type are the reading laboratories produced by SRA, and although these are currently selling well they are still very much a minority method in junior, middle and secondary schools. No doubt many teachers have been deterred by the Americanized spelling, language and content of the earliest imports and by the fact that they were unsupported by any supplementary reading matter. The latter criticism no long applies since the introduction of the Pilot Libraries. Anglicization of the entire series is proceeding and when completed should remove a significant area of complaint by British teachers. The major deterrent continues to be the high initial cost of the basic card material coupled with the (to British teachers) exorbitant price of the expendable individuals pupil's workbooks which are essential to the operation of the scheme. A British rival, Ward Lock Educational's *Reading Workshops,* are also available and are selling at about half the price of the SRA material.

Development of critical reading

This, probably the most important aspect of reading and the ultimate goal of reading instruction and development, is virtually unknown territory in British schools. Historically, the goal of reading instruction has been functional competence only and little has been done beyond this level. What is needed in this area is an upward reorientation of goals towards this end and the training of teachers in techniques and forms of organization which will contribute to its achievement.

A suggested framework for advanced reading instruction

So far this book has been concerned with clearing the ground for a methodology directed towards the accomplishment of the major aims of developing critical, efficient and habitual readers. An attempt has been made to show that neither surviving archaisms nor most current approaches to teaching reading are effective for these purposes. What principles then should form the guidelines for a workable advanced reading curriculum?

Clearly defined aims

First, to attempt too much usually results in achieving too little. For this reason only the three main aims of developing readers who are critical, efficient and habitual are considered relevant for advanced reading instruction. Most textbooks on the teaching of reading suffer from a multiplicity of expressed aims, confusing what is relevant at the beginning stages with what is important at later levels, and entangling short-term goals in a maze of long-term objectives. It is to avoid such confusion of goals that a major premise of this book was stated at the outset, namely that beginning reading has no place in the sort of thinking associated with advanced reading. Before advanced reading can begin in earnest basic competence must be achieved. Once this has been done all teacher activity can then be concentrated and directed towards objectives which are clearly defined and within the capacity of the teacher to realize.

Time

There was once a time when the three Rs dominated the school timetable. I remember when my younger brother first started school. When he came home my mother asked him, 'Well, what did you do at school today? His reply was a curt 'reading, writing and figures!' The next evening a similar question evoked a similar response. On the third day when asked the inevitable question he replied somewhat crossly, 'We did reading, writing and figures. We'll be doing the same tomorrow and the same the day after. So please don't ask me again.' My brother was not normally given to displays of bad temper but was no doubt exasperated on this occasion by what he considered an intolerable lack of perspicacity on the part of adults who could not apparently perceive the nature of an educational system which was transparently obvious to one who had experienced it for only three days.

Times have certainly changed and today, once out of the infant school, the three Rs have been elbowed out of their former privileged position by a multiplicity of innovations. In the junior and subsequent stages of education reading has emerged as the least privileged of the former triumvirate, with a loss of privilege which has gone so far as to rank as sheer neglect.

It is interesting here to consider how time devoted to reading instruction in this country compares with that normally given in the United States. In the United States reading is seen as a continuum and a progression that goes at least to Grade 6 (age twelve) and in some school systems to Grade 12 (age eighteen), with a daily reading lesson as the basis of instruction, with each teacher in each grade, certainly up to Grade 6, having his part (for which he has had lengthy training) to play in the process.

If reading is to be taught at all in the junior and subsequent levels of schooling, time will have to be allocated to it. If it is to be taught well the time allocated will have to be not only sufficient to do what has to be done but will also have to be regular if systematic development is to proceed. What is needed is a daily reading lesson of one hour in all classes from the start of the second junior year onwards in all our junior and middle schools. (Because of the restraints imposed on secondary schools by their peculiar timetabling difficulties the teaching of reading in secondary institutions will be specifically dealt with in a later chapter. However, many of the techniques advocated in subsequent chapters as part of junior/middle school practice are highly suitable for secondary level.) One hour as a proportion of each school day is no more than a suitable index of the basic importance of reading in the school curriculum. During this hour all effort will be devoted to the development of those skills and attitudes which will best promote the aims of producing readers who read efficiently and critically and who love to read both for information and pleasure. Without such a regular allocation of time, reading will be unable to compete for status with those subjects which are already entrenched or with integrated curricula in which reading development is minimized by overattention to interest-orientated or child-centred activities. The rest of the school day will still be available for the incidental application of reading skills to the other curricular areas.

Organization
It is important in the first place to concede the need for a regular daily reading lesson of one hour. However, once such an allocation of valuable time is acquired what matters most is how that time can be

put to the most effective use. The teacher must so organize within that time that each child progressively develops towards becoming more efficient, more critical and more fond of reading. Not all of these things can be done simultaneously, nor can the teacher teach more than one group or individual at a time. Therefore, she must make sure that a majority of children are engaged at quiet reading pursuits each at a suitable level, leaving her free for minority work with groups or individuals. The children too, whether as members of groups or as individuals, whether working with the teacher or on their own, need to be guaranteed freedom from distraction and unnecessary interruption.

The only type of materials which cater for a wide range of individual differences and which enable a child to work not only at his own level but also at his own rate are the multilevel variety incorporated into the SRA Reading Laboratories and the Ward Lock Educational Reading Workshops. The appropriate reading laboratory should occupy the majority of the children purposefully and effectively at the 'quiet pursuits' level for most of the daily hour. This is the most appropriate means of developing the efficiency skills individually and requires a minimum of teacher-control or supervision.

While the majority are thus engaged at the appropriate level of individual work for skill and rate development, the teacher can spend a large proportion of each reading lesson promoting group work and discussion directed either towards the establishment of critical attitudes towards content or intelligent appraisal of the language structures used, or in individual tutorials designed to assess the child's recent and current reading interests and by discussing with him what he reads to encourage deeper insights and guide his further reading.

Subsequent chapters elaborate each aspect of this framewok.

Summary
Surviving archaic methods such as class and group oral reading are ineffective for the purposes of advanced reading instruction, as is the practice of hearing children read individually, an activity which is time-consuming and more appropriate to the beginning stage. Current approaches to reading such as topic and project work are too unstructured and haphazard for purposeful reading development, and when overindulged, as they frequently are, take up valuable time which could usefully be devoted to more systematic advanced reading programmes. Comprehension exercises of the traditional type are rarely at a level above the merely literal and their backward-looking nature renders them ineffective for advanced reading activity, which is essentially active and questioning and more concerned with anticipation and prediction than with passivity and mere recall. What is advocated is a daily reading lesson of one hour for all classes from the

start of the second junior year. The basic skill and rate development will be by individual work with the appropriate reading laboratories, with the teacher reasonably free to work either with groups or individuals at activities specifically designed to further the three major aims of reading extension.

Part 2

Teacher-directed oral group activities

Each of the three chapters in Part 2 deals with a specific group activity. Group methods are stressed for economy and because of the need to counteract a tendency to overindividualize the teaching of reading. This is partly due to a hangover from infant methods associated with look and say approaches and hearing children read, and partly to the heavy load of written activity resulting from incidental approaches to teaching reading, as well as the prevalence of comprehension and vocabulary exercises of the traditional type. Both forms of activity need to be reduced in favour of individual work of the kinds described in Part 3. Each group activity recommended here is teacher-directed and the basic purpose of each is to promote oral discussion arising from silent reading. Personal direction and involvement are essential if the teacher is to maintain responsibility for reading development by preparation, control of ongoing reading behaviour and organization of follow-up activities. The teacher's role in group work is twofold. He has to select and organize the material so that it is always at a suitable level of challenge, stimulating but never overfacing, and structured progressively along a gradient of constantly increasing difficulty. He has also to select and organize the group so that each member derives maximum benefit from the activity. Where discussion and participation are the principal teaching agencies it is obvious that some limitations have to be put on group size. A group larger than a dozen becomes difficult to control if all members are to make contributions and if the discussion is to be kept within reasonable bounds. Groups numbering less than eight give insufficient scope for the presentation of a reasonable range of points of view. Consequently, a group of between eight and twelve is recommended as the optimum size for the procedures to be developed. The more homogeneous the groups, the more the teacher can tailor materials and level of challenge to the group's specific needs. Groups will be formed by a combination of objective reading scores and insightful teacher observation of reading performance. Once the groups are formed the teacher's task is to encourage discussion and to control it at a level which will best achieve the objectives of the particular exercise. For this purpose she would do well to resist all temptations to lead or sway the discussion in any way and to adopt rather the role of an unobtrusive chairman, stepping in only when the discussion threatens to get out of hand or off course and occasionally summarizing objectively the different points of view expressed. In general, she can best promote the purposes of group discussion by confining herself to asking the group the following three things:

1 What do you think?
2 Why do you think so?
3 Will you read out the part which proves it?

The rest can safely be left to the group, provided that each member is given opportunities to make his decisions and occasionally, in the light of adduced evidence, to alter them.

The activities in Part 2 are all of an oral nature, partly because discussion can proceed in no other way and partly to counteract the trend to use writing as an activity which dominates school behaviour and yet is rarely put to use once children leave school. Thus the accent is on language behaviour of a much more useful kind i.e. reading, thinking and speaking, listening. Finally, though the means of learning will be by oral discussion, the major reading tasks will be done silently. Oral reading is not neglected but is in fact enhanced by the opportunities to use it at a purely functional level.

Chapter 3

Group prediction exercises

Critical reading has been defined by Russell (1964) as the application of critical thinking to the reading process. Russell sees critical thinking as a three-factor ability involving an attitude factor of questioning and suspended judgment, a functional factor requiring methods of logical inquiry and problem solving, and a judgment factor of evaluating in terms of some accepted criterion. Group prediction exercises are aimed at developing attitudes appropriate to critical thinking by setting up problems arising from reading which call for the exercise of judgment based on textual evidence.

Basically, the method involves giving the group instalments of reading matter in sequence. After each instalment, which is read silently, the group are invited to make comments on the material in order to predict the major outcomes. Hunches must be supported by evidence from the text, whether stated or implied, and may be either modified or confirmed as the evidence from further instalments comes to light. Though the intellectual excitement and cut and thrust of a group prediction activity is difficult to recapture in cold print, the following account may give some indications of the possibilities of this technique.

I was recently invited to conduct a series of seminars on teaching the higher order skills at an international conference of reading experts. Aware of the high technical ability and width of reading of the audience, I decided to write a short story to guarantee against any possibility of the reading material being familiar to the group. The story was flashed in seven instalments on an overhead projector and a group of ten people was invited to participate in prediction work under my chairmanship. Each instalment remained on the screen until discussion was exhausted. The next section was then screened. The exercise was recorded on tape and comments appear below. The participants are distinguished numerically by the numbers 1 to 10; the chairman is identified by the symbol C.

Instalment 1

The Last Days of Ojukwu
The clouds charged up from the horizon and raindrops spattered in the dusty streets. Then the drops changed into streams and the dust into mud. All that night the rain fell and the next day old Ojukwu left his home on the outskirts of the city and went out to the rice paddies. Ojukwu was only one of a stream of old men and women trudging up and over the ridge down beyond which the paddy fields lay in a deep bowl in the hills. Children laughed and shouted as they raced past their mothers on the way to the planting. Ojukwu tried to remember how many seasons now the old and the very young had gone out like this to the paddies. Was it five years? Or six? It had not always been thus. Before the war came and took all the young men away, it had been they, the young, who had marched singing over the ridge, eager to pack the young shoots into the soft brown mud. The old then had stayed behind preparing the feast and the carnival which would last for days once the rice crop was safely in.

C Well, what do you think?
3 It's probably set in Africa. Ojukwu is an African-sounding name.
5 I disagree. The paddy fields suggest the Far East. And there's the war. It's more likely to be Korea or Vietnam.
6 Yes, I fancy Vietnam. I have the dreadful feeling that all those defenceless children and old people are going to be shot up and napalmed.
C Can you prove that?
6 Oh no! But it's a possibility. There's an air of impending doom. I think it's about Japan. Oddly enough, I only know one Japanese personally and his name is Ojukwu. It may be that the English spelling makes it look African rather than Japanese.
3 I still think it's Africa. The rice paddies are just a red herring to lead us off the scent.
9 The only thing that's certain is that Ojukwu is an old man who is going to die. The title tells you that.
7 Yes. And there's no indication that he's going to die from napalm. More likely a typhoon.
C Can you prove that?
7 Good Lord, no! But some sort of disaster is approaching and I connect it with nature rather than with war. And it's not Africa – Far East certainly.

10 It sounds to me like Vietnam. It says the war has been going on for five or six years.
C   Would any one else like to make a point? What about you sir? (looking at 8).
8   If that rain keeps up the whole lot are likely to be drowned.
C   Is that a firm prediction?
8   No, I take it back. We are given a valley and a collection of helpless people marooned in it by the weather. The country is at war. I think it is Vietnam. Either Communist guerillas or regular forces are going to invade the valley and Ojukwu gets killed in the fighting.
C   We seem to have exhausted the possibilities. May I sum up then so far? We have one lady opting for an African setting, one for Japan. A majority are for the Far East with the strongest contender Vietnam. Ojukwu is going to die. The general feeling is that he will be killed in some kind of military raid, although some sort of natural disaster cannot be ruled out. Should we go on?

Instalment 2
Ojukwu paused at the top of the hill, partly to regain his breath and rest his aching limbs and partly to look at the town spread flat below him in the valley floor. How big it was now, shining with glass and concrete, its streets paved and noisy with traffic. That had not always been thus either. Ojukwu remembered when it had once been a town built of lath and paper, more than once in fact, for earthquakes had flattened it and it had been rebuilt many times. But there had been no serious tremors for years. Even the Sacred Mountain beyond the town, standing white over its blue foothills, had not erupted for years and its customary plume of smoke seemed no more innocuous than that which came from the chimneys of the factories which dotted the city below.

3   Well that alters the whole thing. I've gone off Africa and will settle for Japan.
4   I didn't make any comments on the first paragraph. There seemed so many possibilities. Now I'd say that an earthquake is probable, or a volcano. There hasn't been any sort of seismic activity for years. Why mention that?
8   Obviously as a red herring. To take our minds off the war in Vietnam.
2   No. I think that all that stuff about war is the red herring. We started off with this continual rain turning everything into mud. Now we have earthquakes and volcanoes on the scene. Something elemental I think. And Japan is noted for its earthquakes.

10 No more so than other places in the Far East. I'm still for napalm and either Korea or Vietnam.

9 As I recall, the title was *The Last Days of Ojukwu*. This implies that he may have been a long time a-dying. There isn't anything yet to say that he wasn't.

1 Not necessarily. The events described might take place over several days, but he could still die quite suddenly and violently on the last day. I think he does and I think it has something to do with the volcano. It's the only thing that is actually named specifically. The Sacred Mountain is Fujiyama in Japan. They used to worship it years ago and the older people probably still do.

6 All volcanoes are sacred mountains to primitive peoples. It could be anywhere in the Far East. But no one has mentioned the city. It must have some significance. It could be Saigon. The Vietcong are forever raiding it.

C We seem to have vetted all sorts of possibilities. Africa has dropped out of the reckoning and Japan has picked up a few adherents. There appears to be a rough balance between Japan and Vietnam, or Korea, and between Ojukwu dying either as a result of some cataclysm of nature or of miltary conflict. We've only had hunches so far – no firm predictions. And one interesting speculation that Ojukwu has a long, lingering death. We've obviously not had enough to go on yet. Shall we proceed?

Instalment 3

Ojukwu went on over the ridge and down to the paddy fields. He waded knee-deep in the brown water and worked all day with the other old men and women and the young boys and girls. By evening, half the rice crop had been transplanted. That night it rained without once stopping and Ojukwu was glad that he had not gone back to the city but had stayed with his old friend Tanato in his little farmhouse overlooking the rice fields. It rained all morning as they worked in the fields, but at noon the clouds departed and the sun beat down, but the tender shoots were deep and safe under the brown water in the paddies. It was a pity the sun came out for otherwise Ojukwu might not have resisted his friend's invitation to stay yet another night. And who knows? He might have lived.

7 Well there's obviously no danger of death from storms or hurricanes. The sun is out so he must die when he gets back to the city.

4   It doesn't actually say that he got there. He might be killed on the way.

5   Yet, just within sight of home. A sudden napalm attack and that's that.

9   He's obviously going to die that afternoon. If he had stayed with Tanato he would have lived.

10 'Might have lived' it says. And 'Who knows?' That seems to imply that he could equally have died while staying with Tanato.

1   I've been thinking back to the last paragraph and trying to eliminate some of the possibilities. I think it said the volcano was beyond the city from where Ojukwu was standing. That means the volcano is separated from the rice fields by the city and therefore it must be quite a long way off. For me, that rules out the volcano. An earthquake is still a possibility though.

8   It is. I agree that the volcano seems a little remote. But the country is at war and bombing and shooting must be a probability.

9   We have no evidence at all about the manner of Ojukwu's death. The only near certainty is that it is quite imminent.

C   Should we go on to the next paragraph then?

Instalment 4

But Ojukwu trudged wearily back in the bright sun over the ridge to the town. His son was due for leave and might even be home for the feast. If he did come, how proud Ojukwu would be for had not the Sun God Himself honoured him as a brave flier of the Empire, and how smart he would look in his pilot's uniform with his ribbons and medals and especially the winged star for supreme bravery of the Imperial Air Force. Who knows? That plane which even now he could hear but not see, so high was it, might be bringing home his son, circling above the town ready to glide home to the airfield which lay in the next valley beyond. And so Ojukwu topped the ridge and walked some yards down towards the city and sat down by the side of the road, partly to regain his breath and partly to admire the view. That was the last time Ojukwu saw the city and the last thing but one he ever did see.

7   It's the atom bomb.

8   It is. There's only one plane and it's very high.

4   Yes. It's circling overhead and it's got to fly high to avoid the shockwave.

2   Well it's certainly Japan. No other country in the Far East has an

Imperial Air Force. And the Sun God – that was their Emperor.

7 Yes. Hirohito it was.

9 And the city is Hiroshima.

8 Or Nagasaki. It could be either.

C (to No 8) You've gone off Vietnam then?

8 I have. To introduce the plane at this stage narrows the whole thing down.

10 I think it's the atom bomb now. It's certainly Japan and the various cataclysms seem to have been eliminated – the natural ones that is.

3 It said earlier that the war lasted five or six years. It must have been the last war and this was the bomb that finished it.

C The consensus appears to be almost 100 per cent in favour of the atom bomb. Which city it is is still in doubt. Here's the next paragraph.

Instalment 5

For at that instant there rose from within the shining city a light that was not of this world. It was the light of a million suns in one. It was a light such as Ojukwu had never seen – a great green super-sun. Its light which blinded Ojukwu instantly did not enable him to see that in a fraction of a second it had climbed to a height of several thousand feet, rising ever higher until it reached the clouds, burning earth and sky all around with its dazzling power. Up and up it spread, a great corona of green fire at least a mile across. As it thrust upwards and outwards it changed colour as it grew, from purple to orange, from orange to green, spreading outwards as it shot upwards, and rising as it spread.

4 We were right. It was the atom bomb.

(A general consensus of agreement overwhelmed the Chairman's attempts to maintain order and the rule of only speaking through the chair when requested to do so proved impossible to enforce. However, order was soon restored.)

C We appear to have 100 per cent consensus on the atom bomb. the only thing in doubt is which one. Let's read on.

Instalment 6

A giant cloud surged from the ground and followed the path of the giant sun. In seconds it grew to a giant pillar. Seconds more and a great dome bestrode the pillar, transforming it for an instant into an awesome and unearthly mushroom magnified a million times. Up and up it pushed through the dazzling clouds, up and out beyond them until it reached a height of 41,000 feet, four times higher than Fujyama itself and two miles higher than Everest. It was as though earth and sky had been torn apart by that almighty sun into a great void which the cloud possessed as its own domain.

6 There's the pillar of cloud and the dome.
2 The mushroom cloud. It's the atom bomb without any doubt. and probably Hiroshima – the first one.
C Judging by the number of heads nodding in agreement every-body is sold on Ojukwu being killed by the atom bomb in Hiroshima. Here comes section 7.

Instalment 7
But Ojukwu had died while the cloud still grew. He shrivelled up in the first wave of radiation – he and 100,000 others in Hiroshima that day.

9 We've been led off the secnt by thinking of Ojukwu as an individual and not part of a great mass of people all affected by the same things.
2 No, we led ourselves off the scent. Actually I think we narrowed it down quite well.
10 Yes, about halfway through. It was the solitary plane that did it for me. I went right off Vietnam then.

The brevity of the experiment described above is explained by the fact that within a time allocation of forty minutes the following had to be achieved:

1 The rules of discussion had to be spelled out and agreed, i.e. no one was to speak without the Chairman's consent and all speaking had to be done through the chair.
2 The prediction exercise had to be experienced in full.
3 The methodological aspects and the relevance of the exercise for developing critical-reading had to be fully discussed while the practical experience was still fresh in the minds of the audience.

Consequently, the story was exceptionally brief and devoid of any attempt at characterization. However, it was prepared with the con-straints of time in mind, at a level appropriate to the group for which it was intended, and appeared to achieve its major purpose which was to encourage the participants to deduce in the subsequent dis-cussion the main methodological aspects of group prediction tech-niques. The activity was obviously enjoyed by the participants and there is little doubt that it was dominated more by thinking than by any other aspect of behaviour. All three elements of Russell's critical thinking theory are much in evidence as are many of the subskills identified in Helen Robinson's analysis of the abilities essential to critical reading.

When using this method in schools it is certainly not necessary to write specially prepared material. The reasons for doing so in the particular case described have been explained. Almost any type of material, whether fiction or of a more factual nature, may be used, providing that its content, vocabulary and concepts developed are at a suitable level of challenge to the group concerned. Short stories or fairly self-contained single chapters of books are probably the best kinds of material on which to make a start. If these are fairly brief to begin with the teacher can build up expertise in assessing how long to allocate for the silent reading element and how long for discussion, and can also practise the required unobtrusive techniques of chairmanship essential to the procedure. Fairly brief sessions to begin with are also advisable to enable teachers to test out the organizational arrangements which keep the rest of the class occupied, say at multilevel individual work, without which the group activity itself would be unable to function. In time too, teachers can expect to build up a sizeable body of varied material related to the different levels of the groups for which they are responsible. With practice, whole books can be treated this way, a chapter at a time, and a great deal of the reading associated with the content areas, e.g. science, history, geography, could benefit from such an active, questioning, evaluative approach.

The basic material requirement is that each pupil should have his own copy of the reading matter which will need to be stocked or ordered in sets of a dozen. Also it is essential to control the release of each new instalment to prevent reading ahead to confirm hunches. This is simply achieved by sliding an elastic band over each of the two outer edges of the books being used and thus confining the pages to be read prior to any spell of discussion. When each instalment is completed the pages finished with are slid through the bands to isolate the next passage.

When first using this method, teachers will naturally feel more confident if they themselves are familiar with the material to be read by the children and will probably wish to prepare it by reading it through beforehand. Actually, this is by no means necessary, provided the material is at a readability level which experience has shown to be appropriate to the groups concerned. For example, Schonell's readability ratings for the various Wide Range Readers have proved to be acceptable in practice to experienced teachers. Such controlled material need not be prepared by the teacher herself; in fact, if she can approach it with the same freshness as the pupils in the reading group she can share with them the excitement of the project and reduce the risk of in anyway leading or swaying the discussion. Denied foreknowledge, she can add absolute impartiality to the other attributes of chairmanship.

Group oral prediction exercises can be carried out with almost any age group once basic mechanical competence is achieved. This presupposes the ability to read silently and at some length, along with the essential skimming and scanning skills. Skimming is necessary to isolate key words and phrases, and scanning in order to read out those passages which prove the point being made. To do this oral reading competence is also required. Another important prerequisite is experience of reading different types of material. Without some background of reading experience there might be predictions of a very limited and implausible kind. The participants should have the capacity to enjoy the chosen text unhampered by ineptness in word attack and recognition or by vocabulary difficulties. However, should unexpected vocabulary problems occur, the teacher in such a group situation is particularly advantageously placed to handle them as they arise, drawing on the insights and experience of the members and relating meaning to context in a functional setting. These prerequisites do not mean that advanced groups in top infant classes would not benefit from oral group prediction activities from time to time. However, width of reading for the competent top infant reader should be the major goal, aimed at developing the experience which is implicitly required for the type of interpretative reading which is the basis of prediction work with groups. It is in the junior and subsequent stages that the majority of the children have developed the necessary abilities on which group prediction exercises can build, and it is for those stages that prediction techniques are particularly recommended.

An important byproduct of group prediction work is the potential for teacher growth and development. Few teachers are entirely satisfied with their own attitudes and approaches to group formation, size and treatment, and as ways of working with groups develop on lines that are at once pedagogically sound and consistent with the achievement of clearly defined goals there is constant incentive to refine assessment procedures, both by testing and by observation. Again, as the emphasis is on higher order skills, teachers are obliged to look at reading in new ways. The focus is on skills and attitudes far beyond the beginning level and the result can only be far greater teacher insight into the higher reading and thinking processes. The type of skills required for group prediction activity are particularly suitable for the very good readers at almost any level beyond that of mechanical competence. Perhaps with such a suitable technique now to hand, teachers will seek ways through reading of really stretching the bright child who in the past has frequently been a casualty in overcrowded classes. He has been able to cope with the class work and has often been allowed to do little more than just that, rarely having his sights set on achieving anything approaching his true potential. Average, duller and even remedial groups can also benefit from work of this kind on material at the right level by concentration on the direction of the author's thought rather than on the purely linguistic aspects of the symbols by which the thought is expressed. The accent is on reading between the lines and beyond them rather than merely barking at the X print. Another growth area is likely to be in the field of readability. Teachers seeking and acquiring expertise in group prediction activities are likely to rely less and less on hit and miss methods of relating material to group needs and will tend to seek deeper insights into readability and to demand more precise and practicable measuring instruments than are in use at present.

The emergence of methods such as group oral prediction exercises has obvious implications for teacher training. The colleges will need to extend their courses, which at present are largely concerned with teaching beginning and remedial reading, into the realms of the intermediate and higher order skills. Current changes in school organization which will affect patterns of schooling for many years to come will have to be taken into account. A pattern appears to be emerging of first school, middle school and high school, and what needs to emerge on the reading side is a set of methodologies to fit the coming organizational patterns. Colleges should take the opportunity to offer courses in reading which are differentiated according to whether students are preparing to teach infants, juniors or secondary pupils. Probably one of the best ways of giving students insights into the higher order reading skills is to have them take a course of advanced reading instruction themselves. Some work in group oral prediction at the students' own level could be a useful element in such instruction.

Having discussed the prerequisites for administering group prediction activities and some of the possible results and implications of wider school usage of such techniques, it would be profitable to examine the experiment described above and see in what ways the ability to read such material critically is enhanced by the particular treatment prescribed. In the first place, in the absence of any attempt at characterization, the only clues to the author's thinking were provided by the setting and by whatever mood the author was able to convey. At the very outset the collective experience of the group proves to be a powerful aid to the refinement of concepts and identification with the author's purposes. The false assumption that the story is set in Africa is immediately questioned by other members of the group who produce textual evidence to demonstrate that more important clues than the sound of a name are available. Unique λ personal experience can also be harnesed to group purposes as, for example, the knowledge that Ojukwu was the name of a Japanese Δ person actually known by one of the group. Title and mood are accurately interpreted and both possible outcomes – death resulting from either natural phenomena or war – are supported by evidence from the text.

After Instalment 2 more members of the group opt for Japan (which ultimately proves to be the correct setting) by accurately associating the clue, 'Sacred Mountain', with Mount Fuji. Those who continue to connect the story with the war in Vietnam have reasons which at this stage of the account are perfectly credible. Even the inference that Ojukwu does not have a sudden death is quite valid in view of the plural 'Days' in the title.

The possibilities of storms and volcanic action are eliminated by reference to the text in the third instalment and the final cause of death narrowed down to two possible outcomes. The certainty that the atom bomb was the final outcome was predicted halfway through the story (Instalment 4) with the consensus 100 per cent. What was interesting here was the way in which the supporters of the Vietnam war theory, hitherto perfectly tenable, accepted the alternative view, themselves finding weaknesses in their previous arguments and bowing to superior evidence. The reasoning which led to the common judgment arose from a blend of present evidence (the current instalment), recall and interpretation of clues from previous paragraphs and the background reading experience of the participants. The three final instalments only serve to confirm the major prediction, though interest was maintained to the end by the challenge, which was self-imposed by the group, to ascertain the exact setting (Hiroshima) of the story. Of Helen Robinson's twelve abilities essential to critical reading only two (detecting propaganda and reacting to exceptional diction) were not actually put into effect, but then the story was neither propagandist in nature nor exceptional in its diction.

A most interesting contrast between this approach and traditional comprehension exercises arises from the way questions are both posed and treated. Formal comprehension questions are externally imposed on the reader whose thinking is consequently limited to answering the questions set and no more. There is no motivation to read for any other purpose. In the group prediction approach in response to the question 'What do you think?' a number of self-imposed questions are set up by the group. The questions are set up because they are thought to be important for accurate interpretation and understanding of the author's message. All ideas voiced are subjected to the scrutiny and appraisal of the group and by a process of reasoning and evaluation the trivial and irrelevant are discarded and insight into the major purposes of the author is developed. This is not to say that the main idea is the only thing sought. The supporting details are ferreted out and are in fact the main props used to build up final insight. Some healthy competition is almost inevitable in approaches of this kind and gives a certain spice to the activity which is not available to the lonely struggler working away in isolation at comprehension exercises. In group prediction work each individual is entitled to his point of view, providing that this can be substantiated by evidence from the text, and the necessity to constantly prove points when counter evidence is produced challenges the individual to search through the text ever more deeply. Such constant challenge necessitates constant reading – thinking of an active, questioning, evaluative kind which traditional approaches to reading do not provide.

There are dangers that predictive activity could be abused or misused if teachers are not fully aware that this is a group oral discussion operation concerned with the reading, thinking, speaking and listening aspects of language behaviour.. Therefore, attitudes appropriate to other types of reading teaching are quite unsuitable for group discussion methods. An instance of how the hangover from traditional approaches could adversely affect group prediction work arose recently when a group of American teachers participated in such an exercise and immediately afterwards were led to deduce the most suitable modus operandi, particularly with regard to the role of the teacher. They were persuaded only with some difficulty that the typically American approach of preparing new reading matter by introducing and explaining new vocabulary and the more difficult concepts likely to be encountered before the pupils actually read the material, is totally foreign to group prediction activity. The whole value of such methods is that the vocabulary and concepts are clarified through discussion by the group members themselves and any attempt at preteaching robs the activity of the very atmosphere of challenge which is essential to it. Preteaching in such a case is in fact overteaching and exceeds the unobtrusive chairmanlike attitude which is properly required of the teacher.

A group of British teachers in a similar situation also gave cause for grave concern. Having enjoyed a group prediction exercise at their own level and having agreed with the basic purposes and teaching principles relevant to it, they nevertheless proceeded to point out that various follow-up activities could stem from it. They can indeed, and if one such follow-up turned out to be further reading freely chosen by individual members of the group that would be most desirable. However, it soon became obvious that what the teachers had in mind were writing activities stemming from the material read. This teacher concern for writing is a hangover from project approaches which have contaminated teaching in this country for too long. Teachers are forever seeking new starting points from which the very essence of any stimulus is dragged out to the nth. Can we not be concerned from time to time with starting a job and finishing it within a single lesson? This is the appeal of prediction exercises. Once the main outcomes have been predicted and confirmed, the purpose of the exercise has been achieved. In fact, the sooner this is done the greater the enjoyment and sense of achievement of the participants. The way is then open for activity of a totally different kind in a curriculum which requires both balance and variety. There are already innumerable ways of getting children to write from a starting point of reading. What is needed is a diminution of writing activity in schools in favour of reading-cum-thinking and speaking-cum-listening. Oddly enough, a type of writing which could have some relevance for group prediction work i.e. stories and accounts written by the children themselves to be treated by reading groups as prediction material, did not occur to the teachers as it was not strictly a follow-up activity. If children's own writing occasionally formed the subject matter for oral group work there would be some obvious incentive in writing for such a purpose. And if, as a result, there were some improvement in the low level of credibility which characterizes a great deal of what children write, that would be no mean thing. However, this method is one of a battery recommended to promote thinking through discussion; hence its oral nature should be guaranteed. It is also intended to counter excessive individualization in the teaching of reading and any attempts to introduce writing will tend to weaken that intention. Finally, it is intended as an approach which will bring to the reading lesson, both for the teacher and the child, a real feeling of enjoyment and achievement. Attempts to use the medium as an excuse for written work will, for many children, deprive it of those desirable attributes.

Summary

The aim of group oral prediction exercises is to develop attitudes appropriate to critical thinking by setting up problems arising from reading which are to be solved by the application of logical judgments based on textual evidence. The basis of the method is to release to the group instalments of reading matter in sequence. After each instalment the group are invited to comment on the material read in order to predict the major outcomes. The method is suitable for most types of material, whether factual or fictional, and for almost any age group whose basic reading competence is assured. The teacher's role is that of a chairman, creating conditions for intelligent discussion but not influencing it in any way. The group members decide their own purposes and assess the ultimate truth and validity of their judgments on the basis of textual evidence. Preteaching of the vocabulary and the use of the material for written activities are not recommended.

Possible outcomes of growth in the use of this method are greater teacher competence in group formation and treatment, deeper insights into higher order reading behaviour, more effective methods of stretching brighter children, concentration on reading for meaning rather than on merely decoding for the average and duller pupils, increased interest in readability, improvements in the training of teachers to teach reading, and an upsurge in enjoyment and sense of achievement in reading for both teachers and pupils.

Chapter 4

Group deletion exercises

The previous chapter outlined a method by which the reader can be helped to identify his thinking with that of the author and correctly anticipate the direction in which the author is going. Chapter 4 is also concerned with anticipation, but is directed at the anticipation of the language structures used by the author, both as an aid to fluency and to acquiring the great speed of recognition essential to advanced reading. In the word by word reading characteristic of the beginning reader the text may be likened to a string of beads each of which has equal weight. The result is that accent, pause, stress, elision and all those various devices which the good reader uses to give expression and meaning to what he reads are not brought into play; each word is a new obstacle to be overcome. Thus, by concentrating on each word in isolation the totality of meaning is lost. As the child develops greater language facility and experience he becomes aware that words in isolation are no aid to overall meaning and that, in fact, words generally come together in fairly consistent patterns. The greater the familiarity the reader has with a wide range of language structures, the less he needs to bring word attack skills to bear on his reading and the more he can handle words in meaningful groups at speed. The accomplished reader can interpret clusters of meaning correctly from the most minimal cues and reading becomes largely a matter of intelligent guesswork. Only when the guesses fail to give a satisfactory meaning does the reader then need to call on his reserve armoury, using context first and then, if necessary, word attack resources based on word length, shape and letter position and sequence.

One of the basic aids to correct anticipation is collocation – the tendency of words to pair off with other words. As an instance of this a group of some eighty students were given the adjective 'electric' and asked to write down immediately one noun which could be thus described. The eighty students between them produced only the following nouns: fire, stove, cooker, oven, shock, chair, light and blanket. In their collective experience these are the objects most likely to be qualified by the word electric. Consequently, on reading that adjective all the other words which it could possibly suitably describe are automatically eliminated by the reader's experience. Common experience indicates that the word is likely to be one of the following: fire, stove, cooker, oven, shock, chair, light and blanket. Now suppose that the reading matter describes a man, tired and cold, coming home from work, and goes on 'He put on his slippers and switched on the electric. . . .'. Here the context further eliminates almost all possibilities except fire and thus saves the reader the trouble of even considering the other possibilities in the short list.

Similarly, grammatical considerations eliminate large areas of possible speculation and thereby save time and effort in reading by narrowing the range of anticipations required. For example, in the sentence, 'He had a . . . leg', the word required is limited to an adjective which begins with a consonant, while in 'He had to . . . for the bus', the missing word is obviously a verb.

As convention and grammar limit the reader's range of possible anticipations, they also limit the choice of words available to the writer, so that providing the writer's language experience is not too greatly different from that of the reader, the chances of author and reader being familiar with the same types of language patterns and structures are high, as are the chances of the reader correctly anticipating the particular phraseology used. The reader whose language experience is restricted does not have the means whereby the possibilities of anticipation are narrowed to a small workable range. He is reduced to word by word reading which neglects context, and a whole habit of reading is set in train which effectively cuts out any likelihood of thinking ahead. By concentrating on the print he fails to get the message or gets it by dint of such uneconomic effort as to make the whole thing an irksome chore.

Attempts to enlarge and enrich the children's language experience and to familiarize them with language structures of increasing complexity, have depended on the vocabulary exercise in schools at all levels. Basically, this involves the pupil supplying from a given list the word or phrase which best completes a certain language pattern. This is fraught with all sorts of difficulties. In the first place this is usually done as an individual written exercise. There is no one with whom the child may confer. There is no means of checking that he has made a wrong choice until the teacher marks it wrong. Even if his choice is correct there is no way to confirm this until it is marked right by the teacher. Neither are there opportunities to question why the choices should be limited to the range given or whether, in fact, more suitable words or phrases could be supplied. Such difficulties are bound to arise when the child is on his own with insufficient personal resources to cope with the activity and when the only person asking the questions is the teacher. To correct this situation such tasks should be done as group work rather than individually, and orally rather than in writing. The children can then question each other and use their collective experience to solve common problems.

A highly promising set of techniques is emerging from work on cloze procedure which could revitalize this aspect of exploring the language structures used in reading material. It is based on the deletion of words at regular intervals in a passage and the pupils are invited to supply the missing words. Some idea of what is involved will be gained if readers themselves attempt the following exercises. In each group a complete paragraph is given first to enable the reader to get the main gist and tune in on the author's style and intent. In each second paragraph words are deleted at regular intervals and readers are invited to supply them. In Paragraph B every tenth word is deleted. (The answers are on page 52).

Paragraph A

Joe Taylor left school without ever having learned to read or write. His first venture into employment, as a trainee lavatory attendant, was negatived by his twin disability. He was unable to read the terms of the Borough contract of employment and incapable of even signing his name to it. After all sorts of dead-end jobs he finally became self-employed. He acquired a barrow and set up in the rag and bone business. He prospered and soon exchanged the barrow for a cart and he bought a horse to pull it. While still a young man he went into the scrap metal business and by the time he was married was well on the way to making his first million.

Paragraph B

Years later, as the world famous philanthropist, Lord Taylor, ——[1] was interviewed by Eamon Andrews in the television programme ——[2] *is Your Life*. His career was retraced from its ——[3] beginnings and His Lordship was obviously moved at meeting ——[4] friends who recalled incidents half-forgotten. The growth and ——[5] of his many business interests were also reviewed as ——[6] his many benefactions and the honours which public life ——[7] brought him. The climax came for the viewers when ——[8] interviewer revealed that His Lordship could not read. One ——[9], he suggested, what His Lordship would have achieved if ——[10] addition to all his natural talents he had been ——[11] to read as well. Lord Taylor knew very well ——[12]. He would, he said, have been a lavatory attendant.

Such exercises can be made progressively more difficult by decreasing the intervals between deletions. Readers are invited to try the following exercise in which each seventh word is deleted. (Answers on page 52).

Paragraph C

My earliest experience of teaching adult illiterates came just after the war had finished when I was transferred to the Army Education Corps to help reeducate some of the millions of men who were awaiting demobilization. A great deal of the work involved the organization of discussion groups on current affairs and it was quite pleasant to get about on my motor bike from unit to unit. However, this pleasant way of life was suddenly shattered by an additional assignment, namely to teach an illiterate young guardsman to read each weekday from 09.00 to 09.30 hours. I was given six weeks to get him reading, and if at the end of that time there was no notable success he would not be allowed to remain in the Guards unit to which he was assigned.

Paragraph D

I was petrified. At college before ——[1] war I had been taught nothing ——[2] the teaching of reading. There were ——[3] materials to hand for work at ——[4] level. For days I searched feverishly ——[5] material adult enough to interest my ——[6] yet sufficiently simple to give him ——[7]. At last I alighted on a ——[8] cartoon in which each day a ——[9] lady named Jane took off various ——[10] of clothing for the delight of ——[11] of the Daily Mirror. Among my ——[12] guardsman's earliest sight vocabulary were such ——[13] as 'bust', 'knickers' and 'bra'. From ——[14] we graduated to the sports pages ——[15] company orders. After about a month ——[16] was awakened at an ungodly hour ——[17] my pupil brandishing a letter from ——[18] wife and proudly proclaiming that he ——[19] read it. Thereupon he burst into ——[20] and I joined in too. There ——[21] were, two grown men, sobbing away ——[22] tears of joy. It was the ——[23] of his wife's many letters that ——[24] mates had not had to read ——[25] him, and he answered it himself. ——[26] left me the following week, and ——[27] week after that I was presented ——[28] a handbook which had apparently been ——[29] print for some years. It was ——[30] Canadian Army manual for teaching illiterate ——[31] to read.

Fifth word deletion is correspondingly more difficult. Try these. (Answers on page 52).

Paragraph E

Cloze procedure derives from the term closure used by Gestalt psychologists to describe the tendency to complete missing parts of a pattern. For example, even when given an incomplete circumference we still tend to see a whole circle. Much television advertising makes use of this principle, as in the well known 'Shh. You know who'.

Paragraph F

When cloze procedure is ——¹ to reading tasks the ——² is asked to fill ——³ gap, usually a single ——⁴, which has been left ——⁵ the text. To do ——⁶ successfully the word must ——⁷ to the rules of ——⁸, have the correct meaning, ——⁹ be consistent with the ——¹⁰ and language patterns of ——¹¹ author.

These exercises have been included for the sole purpose of giving teachers some first hand experience of the kind of mental activity associated with deletion exercises. On no account should exercises be given to children in such a manner. Deletion exercises are intended as a group activity. The children are presented with suitably prepared material. Closures are made as a result of oral discussion of all the relevant possibilities. Each participant may suggest a possible solution for each deletion and must be prepared to support his choice by convincing the other members of the group that his suggestion is better than theirs on grounds of grammatical accuracy, correctness of meaning within the appropriate context, and general compatibility with the author's vocabulary and language patterns. Final choices are by group consensus. Not infrequently children supply words which are just as apt as those chosen by the author. They are invariably delighted at such achievements and the teacher-chairman should give them full credit in such cases. When all the gaps have been filled the original text is given and the children compare their choices with those made by the author. Full opportunity should be given to discuss all errors made and the reasons for those errors should be fully brought out in discussion.

The fairly homogeneous group of eight to twelve members is a good teaching unit. With such a group it is easier to provide challenging material at a suitable level. However, eight to twelve children can be a somewhat unwieldy number to handle for this specific type of work and giving each child opportunities to discuss each closure can take a considerable amount of time. In practice, therefore, and in order to introduce a little healthy competition, the group should be divided into subgroups of three or four. Each subgroup arrives at its own consensus independently and after a given time all subgroups come together to discuss their results and compare them with the original text. The postmortems are probably the most valuable part of the activity for it is at this stage that rival views are expressed and contested, errors are discussed, and occasionally discoveries are made that certain solutions are as good as, if not better than, the original choice of word. During the period when each subgroup is working independently at its closures the teacher need not be in direct control. This stage of the activity can be designated 'quiet work' and therefore during this part of the daily reading lesson the teacher can be available for work at activities with other groups or with individuals.

She must, however, be available to chair the postmortem when all the subgroups come together to discuss their results.

It is possible that deletion exercises may initially not be so popular with teachers as prediction activities, owing to the amount of preparation required. However, if teachers are really keen to extend the language experience of their pupils and to give them opportunities to think about and discuss the ways in which language is used, they will find their time well spent in building up suitable material for the different groups for whom they are responsible. Few approaches can rival this in sustained, active, productive pupil response. To begin with the material should be written on the blackboard and should consist of very short passages with every tenth word deleted. In time teachers will come to know at what levels to pitch the material to suit groups of different ability and how to allocate time, and how much time, to the activity. As expertise grows, material of the types and levels found by experience to be most suitable could be duplicated and a stock of exercises, graded along a continuum of gradually increasing difficulty, built up. As with prediction exercises there is a place too for occasionally using children's own writing as the material for group deletion work. In fact this would make an excellent starting point. Not only is there some incentive in writing for so useful a purpose but the language patterns used in children's writing are more likely to be familiar to the other children reading them than those of adult authors.

Group oral deletion exercises have no common ground with the time-honoured attitudes associated with teacher-designed exercises in 'filling in the blanks'. In the latter activity the teacher, in preparing or selecting the material, knows exactly what should go into the blanks and has that in mind at the outset. It is usually a correct spelling or a word with a certain meaning, either of which has usually (though unfortunately not always) been the subject of recent teaching and the answers to be provided are usually related in some way. Blank filling in these cases is a testing rather than a teaching situation and is associated with spelling, vocabulary and comprehension exercises of the traditional kind, to be done in writing as an individual assignment. Readers will no doubt be familiar with blank filling to test the following:

Spelling
Write in full the incomplete word: The captain rec . . . . the cup from the headmaster.

Vocabulary
Use each of the following verbs to complete one of the sentences below: appear, disappear, ascend, descend.
1 To   means to go up.

2 To   means to come into view.
3 To   means to go down.
4 To   means to go out of sight.

Comprehension
Read the following:
We had a lovely day by the sea. The weather was warm and there was a slight breeze blowing. The sea was very calm and we had an enjoyable swim while Mummy and Daddy dozed in their deckchairs. In the afternoon we hired a boat and fished for mackerel. It was our first experience of sea fishing.
Now write in each gap the correct word used in the story:
1 An   is what happens to you.
2 The swim was   .
3 Another word for wind is   .
4 When the sea is not rough it is   .
5 Our parents   in their deckchairs.

In these examples the pupil activityinvolved is quite undemanding. The design of the exercise will result in thinking of the most convergent kind. The teacher wants a certain response and the form of the material limits pupil activity to supplying that response. The response is the object of the exercise, not the pupil activity or thinking by which the response is produced.

In group oral deletion exercises the regularity of deletion (e.g. every tenth word) applied to the irregular patterns of language results in an almost random sampling of the various parts of speech and an almost infinite variety of possible applications. With every deletion a new situation arises which requires the participant to set up a new hypothesis. This is evaluated in the light of his own experience, the rules of grammar, the correctness of meaning within the appropriate context and the structure associated with the author's particular way of thinking and the ways in which that thinking is expressed. Each hypothesis must be questioned and if on any one criterion it remains implausible, new hypotheses must be established. Further questioning and evaluation, constant criticism and logical reasoning are applied until the area of search is reduced to what is strictly credible and appropriate. All evidence adduced to support the final hypothesis must be presented to the other members of the group who subject each possibility to their collective critical thinking and whose counter evidence is a constant challenge to refine one's thinking and either produce more powerful reasons for retaining one's point of view or for altering it in the light of evidence of greater validity. Although the ultimate correctness of the final response matters, the fact that other responses may be even more apt than those chosen by the author encourages

47

divergent thinking. The correctness or otherwise of the final choices is not the major goal of the exercise. The means by which the choices are arrived at, the active problem-solving nature of those means, the level and extent of critical thinking arising in discussion, the promotion of questioning attitudes appropriate to critical reading, and situations in which critical reading can be exercised – these are the outcomes for which the group oral discussion approach to deletion is recommended.

Having in mind the different abilities of the various groups in any given class, it is obviously useful to suggest simple but effective ways by which deletion exercises can be graded in difficulty. At the lower levels of ability structural prompts of various kinds can limit the number of possible choices available. Though such limitations invariably result in convergent thinking it is essential, especially at the initial stages, to pitch the material at levels which challenge while giving some success. Some useful byproducts likely to arise from the presentation of certain cues are increased skill in word attack and more careful scrutiny of word shapes and letter sequences leading to improvement in spelling. Six suggestions for a simple gradation of deletions at the tenth word level follow.

1 *Word shape plus initial letter*

The battle raged all day. The Indians charged time[1] ▨▢▢▢ ▢▢▢ time but the fort held out. Some soldiers were[2] ▣▢▢▢▢ and many wounded, but always there was someone to[3] ▣▢▢▢ the place of those who fell. Within the compound[4] ▣▢▢▢ after fire was started by flaming arrows but the[5] ▣▢▢▢▢ and children of the settlers were always ready with[6] ▣▢▢▢ buckets, constantly replenished at the pump, to put these[7] ▣▢▢

In this example powerful clues are provided – the initial letter, the number of letters, the shape of the words and especially indications as to which letters are ascenders or descenders. The provision of such a number of clues drastically limits the range of possible hypotheses and is therefore suitable at initial stages with less able groups. Example 2 below is made more difficult by the omission of the initial letter clue.

2 *Word shape only*

The men settlers stood shoulder to shoulder with the [1] ▢▢▢▢▢▢▢ at the battlements. They too suffered heavy losses. The[2] ▢▢▢▢▢▢ lost no time in mourning but took up the [3] ▢▢▢▢▢ of their husbands who had died, while other tended [4] ▢▢▢ injured. or reloaded the rifles of those who, though [5] ▢▢▢▢▢▢▢ , could still fire a gun. Thus, though innumerable attacks[6] ▢▢▢▢ mounted, the attackers never once broke through and towards[7] ▢▢▢▢▢▢▢ they broke off the fight.

Answers to Exercise 2
1 soldiers 2 women 3 guns 4 the 5 wounded 6 were 7 evening.

The second deletion in this example is an interesting case of when another word could on all valid grounds be substituted for the original choice. The word 'wives' in this case is as apt as 'women'. If the deletion here had been entire and no structural prompts provided, the word 'womenfolk' would have been equally valid and a discussion on the connotations of all three possible words would be an interesting possibility.

3 *Initial letter plus word length.*

As is evident in the previous example, ascenders and descenders give a word a distinctive appearance and are therefore a powerful aid to recognition. This aid is withdrawn in the example below, although the indication of the number of letters in each word and the provision of the initial letter still give considerable help to the less able in limiting the range of possible choices.

As the gun smoke cleared away, the defenders were [1]a . . . to take stock of their position. Though their own [2]l . . . . . had been severe, those of the enemy were frightening. [3]T . . Indians had borne away their wounded but a vast [4]n . . . . . of their dead still lay where they had fallen [5]a . the approaches to the fort. Their horses too had [6]u . . . . terrible slaughter and many, not yet dead, writhed in [7]a . . . . . Though ammunition was low the Commander ordered compassionately that [8]t . . . should be shot to spare them further suffering.

Answers to Exercise 3
1 able 2 losses 3 The 4 number 5 at 6 undergone 7 agony 8 they.

Exercise 3 provides a good example of the convergent nature of the thinking resulting from the provision of structural prompts. Because of the form of the prompts given, no solutions other than the original choices are admissible. Had the deletions been entire and no prompts given at all, the following alternatives at least may have been initially acceptable: for able – enabled; for undergone – suffered; for agony – anguish; for they – these. In the final analysis whether the alternatives are in fact as acceptable as the originals would require considerable discussion and a detailed examination of the text.

4 *Word length only*
In the following exercise the only clue given is the number of letters in the missing word.

49

Inside the fort the lull in the fighting was [1].... for all sorts of purposes. There was time to [2]...... food, though many, too exhausted to eat it, fell [3]..... at their posts. The wounded were carried to shelter [4]... their wounds were dressed. For the dying there was [5].... for a last look at their loved ones before [6]..... took them mercifully away.

Answers to Exercise 4
1 used   2 prepare   3 asleep   4 and   5 time   6 death.

5 *Entire deletion*
Here no structural prompts of any kind are given. Uniformity of presentation is guaranteed by making each gap say one inch long. Solution depends on accurate anticipation within the limits of the appropriate context. Grading of examples is, of course, possible by either increasing the frequency of deletions as in Paragraphs B, D and E earlier in this chapter or by selecting material of gradually increasing complexity.

Masking
Masking is a method of partial deletion which obviates the need for the preparation and duplication of material by using existing printed matter. Sets of old books which have outlived their traditional usefulness could be given a new lease of life if used for this purpose. Words to be deleted are obliterated in accordance with whatever system or structural prompts is required. For example, the word 'after' could be treated thus:

The latter form of masking is the nearest approach to complete deletion. But, though the obliteration is total thus eliminating letter and word shape cues, indications as to the length of the word in relation to other words in the text, remain. The children themselves could be usefully employed in masking texts according to the teacher's directions. Whole books, suitably treated, could be progressively graded, each chapter being made more difficult than the preceding one, either by decreasing the provision of structural prompts or by increasing the frequency of deletion. It should of course be borne in mind, regardless of the convenience of using ready made material, that masking results more in convergent thinking than does specially prepared material in which the deletions are complete. On a practical note, felt pens and ball point pens do not obliterate most printed texts satisfactorily. Their degree of blackness is inferior to that of printer's ink. Therefore, fixed black Indian Ink is recommended for masking print.

It is hoped that schools will adopt much more widely the sort of group and oral discussion methods, whether for prediction or deletion exercises, so far outlined here. Both appear to have important devices built in to the reading activity which are concerned with anticipating respectively the outcomes suggested by the author's thinking and the patterns of language in which that thinking is expressed. At the junior and middle school levels, where the majority of the children are with the same teacher for the greater part of each day, these oral activities at group level give challenge and variety to the ploys which are basic to reading improvement at those stages of schooling, and to that extent should render both teaching and learning more pleasurable. At the secondary stage reading advancement in the past has been bedevilled by the rigid timetabling necessitated by specialist teaching approaches. Where reading has had any attention at all, it has been considered part of the specialist province of the English teacher, but more usually of the remedial department, and therefore of no concern to the other specialist departments in the school. This is a totally outmoded view of how reading extension should be tackled. All teachers, whatever their subject, depend to a great extent on the ability of their pupils to read. Each subject teacher is a specialist within his own field and he, more than specialists in other areas, knows what is required to read expertly in his chosen subject. He is familiar with the vocabulary and language structures peculiar to the subject and also with the interpretation of nonliteral material such as maps, charts, tables, diagrams and graphs associated with his specialism. He also has expert knowledge of the concepts basic to his subject and the stages by which those concepts grow and are refined. He is familiar with a wide range of supporting material leading to further reading and study, both to reinforce previous learning and to stimulate future growth. With all these qualifications it is idiotic for the specialist to delegate to other departments, who lack his particular expertise, the task of training pupils to read his subject. Each teacher is capable of teaching his own subject reading without altering the subject-orientated approach or the timetabling essential to it. He can teach it within his usual subject periods. Insofar as he is concerned to develop in his pupils critical, questioning attitudes to the subject, with thinking the dominant activity, the type of oral group discussion methods advocated here, employing both prediction and deletion exercises, are particularly suitable techniques for subject teaching at secondary level.

Summary
Group oral deletion aims to help the reader to identify his thinking with that of the author by anticipating the language patterns by

which that thinking is expressed. The basis of the approach is the deletion of words at regular intervals, the reader having to supply the missing words. These must conform to the rules of grammar, have the correct meaning, be appropriate contextually and generally be in tune with the language patterns typical of the author. Choices made must be substantiated in discussion against these criteria. Exercises can be graded in difficulty, simpler treatment for the less able being made possible by the provision of structural prompts. More complex levels are achieved by progressively eliminating such cues and by increasing the frequency of deletions. The method is suitable for introducing variety in the recommended daily reading lessons in junior and middle schools and for work in the content areas by specialist teachers at the secondary stage.

Answers to deletion exercises

Paragraph B
1 he 2 This 3 earliest 4 old 5 extent 6 were 7 had 8 the
9 wondered 10 in 11 able 12 indeed.

Paragraph D
1 the 2 about 3 no 4 this 5 for 6 pupil 7 confidence 8 strip
9 young 10 items 11 readers 12 young 13 words 14 this 15 and 16 1 17 by 18 his 19 could 20 tears 21 we 22 with
23 first 24 his 25 to 26 He 27 the 28 with 29 in 30 a 31 soldiers.

Paragraph F
1 applied 2 reader 3 a 4 word 5 in 6 this 7 conform 8 grammar 9 and 10 style 11 the.

Chapter 5

Survey/Study
Question
Reading/Reviewing/Review

Group oral SQ3R techniques

Surveying

The purpose of this chapter is to introduce a study strategy suitable for application to any of the content areas. Surveying, which is the first stage in the strategy, enables the reader to extract from the reading matter the largest amount of information in the shortest possible time. This is done by a rapid initial reading of those areas of the reading matter which are likely to yield the most important information. In practice these are usually found to be the illustrations, the title, the first sentence and the last paragraph. Surveying rarely takes longer than one minute, but within that time the reader can expect to acquire an increased interest in the reading matter and an increased ability to concentrate on it. In addition, he will be directed to think about what he already knows of the subject and to apply that knowledge to his reading. The reader who surveys a chapter intelligently, rapidly builds up a mental framework of that chapter before he actually reads it. He then goes on to read it in full to fill in the gaps in the content.

I propose to take in turn each of the major surveying cues – illustrations, title, first sentence and last paragraph – and to work out the role each plays in contributing to rapid understanding of what is about to be read and especially to the identification of the main outcomes and the purposes of the author.

Illustrations

A picture is worth a thousand words. Where reading matter is illustrated, the pictures should be 'read' silently by the group, whose findings are then discussed as the first step towards understanding a passage or chapter. If the illustrations are at all relevant they can be expected to yield important clues about the subject – its setting, both in time and place; the main characters, their age, sex, appearance, characteristics and activities. To study the pictures on a basis of oral group discussion gives opportunities to refine the insights of the group and to develop collectively the mental set appropriate to the forthcoming reading.

Title

The title should be the most important indication of what the reading matter is about. Each member of the group should have an opportunity to state what the title means to him, and to suggest, bearing in mind the way the title is phrased, in what ways the material is likely to be developed. If the title is too terse to indicate the likely development of the ensuing text, (e.g. only a single word such as 'Rocks'), pupils should be trained to rephrase the title as a question e. g. What are rocks? What do I know about rocks? How do the pictures I have just read suggest how the subject is to be treated? Discussion of this kind helps point the group towards the direction in which the author is going. The readers are active and anticipatory and are already tuning-in to the author's wavelength. Such discussions also generate confidence in the group's ability to understand the forthcoming reading. At this stage of group surveying activity, and especially when the pupils are in the early stages of acquiring expertise in surveying skills, the teacher should take every opportunity to point out that as readers they are rarely starting from scratch. They already know something (and at times a great deal) about the subject of the reading matter. To prove this point teachers should constantly cite instances which have just arisen when insights were developed at the stages when pictures and title were subjected to group scrutiny and discussion. The main point to be made, of course, is that readers bring a great deal of themselves to the activity of reading, and that their own past experience, whether vicarious or first hand, must be constantly drawn on and related to what the author is saying.

First sentence

The opening sentence, especially with factual material, usually introduces the area of study by expanding and developing the title, and also frequently indicates the author's intended mode of attack, though this may be more often implied than actually stated. Discussion of the implications of the first sentence, in conjunction with the insights already gained from critical appraisal of the picture and title clues, is a powerful aid to correct anticipation of the major issues and an important element in the tuning-in process.

It is important at this stage to attempt to identify whatever bias the author may bring to his treatment of the subject. Reading newspaper and magazine articles is a fruitful area of reading, particularly for groups in secondary schools. However, much that is written in newspaper and magazine articles has a propagandist slant. When surveying such material discussion should be centred on such questions as: What is the author's purpose in writing this? Where is he trying to lead me? In the same way biographers are noted for a tendency to glorify their subject; biographies therefore require a certain objectivity on the part of the reader.

With more complex material, as in the content areas in the secondary field, many texts contain section headings and subheadings. These are powerful indicators of the main direction of the author's thinking and should be subjected, in sequence, to group scrutiny and discussion, once the insights developed from the opening sentence have been acquired.

Last paragraph

The last paragraph usually summarizes the main points of a chapter and gives the author his last chance to emphasize whatever slant he may have adopted towards the subject. Consequently, when groups have read (silently) the last paragraph, they are in a position to evaluate the degree of accuracy with which they predicted the major outcomes on the basis of discussion of the initial survey of pictures, title and first sentence (and section and subheadings if available). They have learned a great deal about the passage before they have actually read it to fill in the gaps in their learning and achieve full understanding. However, before going on with the business of reading the passage in full, it is important to consider a process which is inseparable from surveying and accompanies it automatically, and which is indispensable for anticipation and comprehension of the text. This is the process of questioning.

Questioning

When the reader surveys, he finds it almost impossible to prevent questions coming into his mind. When looking at a picture for example, he can hardly help asking such questions as: Who are these people? What are they doing? Where do they live? When did these things happen? Why are they doing this? The fact that he is asking questions means that he is seeking answers. In the first place readers supply their own in a tentative way. These are the first hypotheses formed about the reading matter. The reader will want to read on either to confirm his hunches or to modify them as the reading proceeds.

When reading the title the reader will ask: What is this about? What do I know about this already? What is the writer trying to tell me? What new knowledge am I likely to learn about this?

Some of these initial questions will probably be answered when the first sentence is read. It is equally likely that given those answers, further questions will arise. For example, on being told by the author that he intends to write about a certain matter for certain purposes, the reader might then ask: But why have those particular purposes? Where is he leading me? Why is he going to tackle it in this way? What slant does he have? Has he an ulterior motive? Haven't I read something like this before? What was it? And who wrote it?

Even at the last stage of the surveying process, i.e. having read the last paragraph, questions continue to stream into the mind: Why should he end on that note? What evidence has he for such a conclusion? How credible is all this? Such questions impel the reader to a really deep reading of the text in full. The inquiring reader wants answers and he will read the text very thoroughly to find them.

At each stage of the survey process the teacher should aim to bring out for discussion all questions which members of the group consider relevant for full understanding of the reading to come. She could, of course, ask the questions herself, or use a textbook in which the author himself has set questions. However, questions asked by the individual are more important and tend to make a greater impression than those which are externally imposed. Therefore it is important that the pupil reads and studies with a questioning attitude. In group oral surveying activities it is essential for the participants to discuss all questions raised and to decide which questions appear to be the most important for revealing and understanding the major issues. Thus, when the actual first reading takes place, the reader knows what he is looking for, and is motivated to find it.

This purposeful reading may be usefully contrasted with the type of reading assignment all too frequently set to pupils in many of our junior and secondary schools, e.g. 'Read chapter 5'. With such a vague assignment the pupil has no specific targets to aim at and no particular questions to answer. Having read the chapter he is unable to recall anything of importance and he has the most confused notions of its sequence and development. Worse, the reader has only become vaguely aware of what he has read when he has finished reading it: Such a reader is handicapped by always having to come up from behind rather than from a position of strength from which he can subject the reading matter to a full-blooded frontal assault. Those teachers who set such vague reading assignments regard the reader more as a sponge, whose only function is to soak up indigestible information, than as an active, questioning human being, reacting to his reading in a challenging, critical way, and spurred by curiosity to refine his insights from the base of his own unique experience. Rather than set vague assignments of the 'Read chapter 5' variety, teachers would do better to suggest, 'Survey chapter 5, and we will discuss what we think about it in a couple of moments.'

The survey-question stages of the study process should be treated as a group oral discussion activity, the purpose of which is to make the pupils used to effective previewing whenever study-type materials are to be read. The group training in SQ techniques should be so thorough and systematic that readers automatically apply them to all new material when reading individually. The SQ stages of study are the essential first two steps in a five-fold strategy; the remaining three are reading, reviewing and reciting. Each of these latter steps will now be examined individually. The interrelationship of these steps will be discussed. Hopefully the insights gained will be applied by competent readers in junior and secondary schools to all suitable reading matter and result in considerable gains in reading efficiency.

Reading
Having surveyed the reading matter and set up certain questions, the next step is to read the passage in full in order to find the answers. In finding answers the active reader will think of further questions. He must do this, challenging the writer at every point, not from mere cussedness or disbelief, but to ensure that he reads with maximum comprehension. As he reads he will read first to identify the main idea, then the details that support it. Next he will attempt to identify the author's purpose and then seek to interpret it. In order to fill in the gaps in the framework which the initial survey has provided, he will look for a sequence of events and attempt to analyse relationships of cause and effect, and of similarity and difference. Pertinent questions at the gap-filling stage could be: Are these facts or the writer's opinions? Why did this happen? What occurred as a consequence? What came first? How are certain characters and situations alike? How are they different? In asking and answering such questions at the reading stage, the reader is evaluating what he reads and exercising and developing the subskills of critical reading-thinking. For the older pupils in secondary schools it might be a very useful exercise to read with the Robinson subskills as a checklist to be used systematically at the reading stage of SQ3R. How effectively the subskills have been put to use will become apparent during the oral discussion which follows the detailed silent reading of the passage. During such discussion the teacher is favourably placed to direct the attention of the pupils to certain subskills which may not have been put to use or which could have been exercised more profitably. In time, the feedback resulting from discussion of the use of the Robinson subskills checklist, and its constant application to a wide range of reading matter, should result in an increased awareness on the part of the pupil of the range of strategies available to him and of their power to help him to extract maximum value from what he reads.

Flexibility at the reading stage.
The discussion following the silent reading stage should also indicate the degree of flexibility of reading rate which the children are developing. After reading, there should be opportunities for each participant to consciously analyse his reading behaviour from the point of view of flexibility. In discussion it could emerge, for example, that some parts of a chapter were easy and were therefore read very rapidly. Some parts, because they were more difficult, had to be read more slowly. Some sections may have been read again and again in

order to understand the meaning of unfamiliar words. Some words, despite much rereading, may still not have been clear, and may have been jotted down to be looked up at the end of the silent reading period. The teacher, in such discussions, is ideally placed to comment on such variations in rate and to lead his pupils to greater awareness of the need to change gear according to conditions on the reading road. Pupil purposes, as well as the nature of the material, are useful regulators of reading rate. Teachers can make much of pupils' comments such as 'I read this bit very quickly because I didn't think it very important', or 'I read this very carefully because it was in italics'. Such discussion has a two-fold value: the pupil not only increases his knowledge and understanding of the reading content, he also becomes aware of himself as a reader and develops insights both into his own reading strengths and weaknesses and into the complex process of reading itself.

Eye movements at the reading stage

The major emphasis of this book is on the thinking aspects of reading. However, reading starts with seeing, and readers can increase not only their reading rate but also their powers of comprehension if they learn to use their eyes efficiently when reading. Children are surprised and interested to learn that, when reading, their eyes do not move in a continuous line of vision along a line of print. Rather, they move by fits and starts, pausing on one word or group of words, then moving to another group, where they pause again. The pauses are termed fixations. It is only during the fixations that reading occurs. The children can easily check these phenomena by observing each other's eye movements when reading.

A slow reader may be slow for two reasons. First, he may make so many fixations that he cannot group the words into phrases or meaningful groups (thought units) and thus reads each word or even part of a word as a separate entity having no relationship with other words or parts of words in the context. Such readers have a limited eye span, i.e. their eyes take in very little print during each fixation. Consider the line of print below in which the fixations made by a certain reader are indicated by vertical strokes and the order of the fixations by the numbers above them:

```
      6  3  2  5 1 4    7    8    9   10    11    12  13
     |The s|ow |rea|der | mak|es |many| fix|ations |per |ine.|
```

Contrast the above with the eye movements of a good reader reading the same line of print:

```
            1                        2                3
     The  slow  reader |makes  many  fixations |per  line.|
```

A second reason for slowness in reading is the excessive duration of the fixations. In the sample line below, the slow reader not only makes a considerable number of fixations but pauses a long time on each one. The numbers below the vertical strokes indicate the time in seconds of each fixation:

The	slow	reader's	pauses	are	too	long.
1.2 1.1	1.2	0.7 0.8 1.0	0.9	1.0 1.0	1.1	0.7

Contrast the above with the performance of a good reader on the same material:

The	slow	reader's	pauses	are	too	long.
		0.4			0.3	

The examples show that reading is slowed down if too many fixations are made or if the pauses are too long. In order to read faster, the eye span must be increased and the pauses shortened, i.e. the fixations per line must be fewer and shorter.

It is possible to train readers to decrease the frequency of their fixations by concentrating on reading in thought units rather than word by word. A thought unit is a phrase or meaningful word grouping. In the line below, the thought units have been separated by vertical strokes and a dot has been placed over the centre of each unit:

You read better | and faster | when you read | in thought units.

The eyes see by first focusing on the centre of an object and then fanning out in all directions. This can be demonstrated to children by getting them to move their eyes from one dot to another along the sample line of print above. Not only will they see the dots, but within a fraction of a second they will see the words in each fixation as well. Reading in thought units is an essential visual-cum-thinking reading skill which can be practised by first reading a paragraph within the reader's comprehension and then marking off the thought units as in the sample line above. A dot is then placed above the centre of each thought unit as a guide for the eyes. There are few readers in our junior and secondary schools who could not make important gains in reading efficiency as a result of such activity.

Reviewing
If study strategies were restricted to the surveying, questioning and

reading stages, the reader could possess a great deal of information which could well prove ephemeral. Further steps in the study process are necessary to reinforce what has been learned so far and to counteract the effects of forgetting. The first of these further steps is the stage of reviewing, which is the second R in the SQ3R study method.

Flexibility in reviewing
Reviewing, as with reading, calls for a certain amount of flexibility on the part of the reader. Depending on the simplicity or complexity of the material and on the purposes of the reader, reviewing can be done with varying degrees of intensity. With simple material, in which the vocabulary and concepts developed are familiar to the reader and of no great importance to him personally, reviewing would take its simplest form, that of reimpression. This is no more than reviewing by rereading. Symbolical reviewing is a much more purposeful operation directed towards the application of what has been learned. Symbolical review encourages thinking, assimilation, and integration and organization of the material learned. Thus between the extremes of reimpression and symbolical reviewing there is a whole gamut of possible strategies available to suit the reader's different purposes: for example a reader may think about a part of a chapter; read it through again; close the book and see how much of the chapter can be recalled; leaf through the chapter slowly, recalling the main ideas evoked by each subheading; think how these ideas are related to form the main idea of the chapter; outline the chapter in brief notes; prepare questions for other members of the group to answer or discuss; underline important passages in the book itself and annotate them. Whichever techniques or combinations of techniques are used, it is important that:

1 Reviewing should be done as soon as the chapter is read.
2 It should always be an exercise in critical reading-thinking.

Importance of reviewing
Pupils should be trained to regard reviewing as very much more than a casual rereading of materials. It should result in an extension and reorganization of what has been learned. Material should be critically reexamined with a view to integrating its content and to acquiring deeper insights and useful generalizations.

Skimming and scanning at the reviewing stage
Skimming is a special kind of reading skill which is put to its most effective use when reviewing. Children can practise this skill by being given the task of finding certain words in a dictionary or specific numbers in a telephone directory. When skimming, the eyes move

rapidly down the page, picking up certain directional clues but ignoring any facts or information irrelevant to their purpose, until they have located the word or number required. Then they stop and read the word or number carefully. This final intensive reading is known as scanning.

When studying an article or chapter to find the name of a character, a date, a place, or a main idea, the eyes move swiftly until they come to a key word or group of words. This key area may indeed yield the information required, or it may give the signal to stop and scan to find out what is needed.

Oral group work at the reviewing stage

Systematic practice in reviewing can most profitably be given on a group basis. The various reviewing strategies could be applied to material of different types and for different purposes. Discussion after each session of practical activity should lead the pupils to growing awareness of their own reading strengths and weaknesses. The ultimate goal of such practice and discussion is automatic transfer of this skill to their own study habits, and consequently a permanent gain in reading efficiency.

Reciting

Reciting tests how well the reading matter has been learned and understood. Basically it can take two forms. It can be the self-recitation of the motivated reader who, without looking at the book, attempts to reconstruct in his own words what has been read. He sets himself the task of relating the material to his previous reading and to his past experience and of answering the questions he has set up during the surveying stage. Several strategies are available to him: for example he can verbalize what he has learned simply by talking to himself; jot down key words and phases in note form; expand such notes into a more continuous outline; or explain or report what he has read to others. The ability to explain to others, in one's own words, what one has learned is a good test of one's own understanding of the material. Recitation can also be externally imposed as when teachers, concerned that important material is thoroughly learned, set specific tasks which are directed to that end. Such directed recitation could include the following: requiring the pupils to provide a written summary or report; writing an essay; taking a test on it; or answering questions only. Whichever method is used, recitation should indicate to the learner whether he has learned what he needs to know. If he has not, the need for further reviewing is clear. Certainly, with important material, brief notes should be written immediately after reading the section or chapter. Notes are a considerable aid to retention of what has been learned.

Importance of recitation

Recitation helps the learner to economize on reading time. Having surveyed, questioned, read and reviewed the material, he is in a position to attack it for its essential meaning and knows where the key areas are for this purpose. He is thus enabled to eliminate the trivial and irrelevant. His powers of memory and of concentration are also improved. The main values of recitation are that mistaken ideas can be corrected and where understanding is defective the reader can be directed to those areas which require greater emphasis or effort. Recitation also enables the learner to be clear about his own goals and objectives. In addition, he is led to conceptualize what may have been a mass of discrete information into an organized system of meaningful relationships. Important byproducts of recitation are increased personal confidence on the part of the learner (such as when he is able to recall and apply information at a later date) and the prestige that increased ability to contribute to group or class discussion confers.

Oral group work at the reciting stage

As with each other step in the SQ3R process there appears to be a good case for some systematic graded practice in recitation. Practice in the various strategies available, each followed by discussion of the value to the individual and to the group of the different methods attempted, should consolidate the efficiency skills and give the reader a useful repertoire of reciting techniques.

Importance of systematic instruction in SQ3R

The emphasis of this chapter so far has been on the oral discussion by reading groups of the five separate stages of SQ3R, following practical activity at each of these levels. However, as expertise grows and pupils recognize the value of each separate stage, there is a need for regular practice to integrate the separate processes and for the application of SQ3R to individual assignments. Thus there should be a gradual change of emphasis from group oral to individual written assignments in order that pupils may read more efficiently and learn more effectively. The SRA *Reading Laboratories* have made important contributions to such regular and systematic practice and have considerably simplified the reading teacher's task by providing an extensive range of graded material and appropriate reading experiences.

Further applications of SQ3R

So far the application of SQ3R to articles and single chapters of books only has been stressed. If the early material is fairly self-contained and not too lengthy, both teachers and pupils can get off to a good start with practice on group lines with the goal of eventual application of SQ3R to individual study habits. However, as the children get into the secondary stage and the subject specialist teaching approach becomes dominant, a great deal of the work depends on the pupils' ability to make good use of textbooks in each of the content areas and to extract maximum value from recommended further reading. This calls for an ability to handle whole books (not merely articles or chapters) efficiently and pupils could benefit from some systematic instruction in the structure of textbooks and in the application of SQ3R methods to longer recommended supporting material.

The structure of textbooks
Most textbooks follow the same general pattern, a fact which facilitates instruction in their use, whatever the specialism. The purpose of such instruction is to help the pupil to make good use of the textbook and to understand how its different parts may contribute to his learning and understanding of the subject.

A great deal of information can be gleaned from the title page alone. The title itself and the way in which it is phrased often give important clues as to the author's purposes in writing the book in the first place. Teachers might do well to explain, in this context, why they choose certain textbooks in preference to others in the same general field. Pupils should also know not only the name of the author, but also his background, experience and qualifications for writing the particular work. They should also understand the importance of knowing the dates of the different editions of an original work. In some subjects the growth of knowledge has been so swift as to make early editions virtually useless. There will be greater confidence in the textbook if pupils know that theirs is the latest edition, or one that has been revised in the light of new knowledge or to suit a particular approach. In this respect, teachers would do well to explain how, in general, the textbook is to be used in relation to the particular course of study being pursued, and here the author's preface or introduction should be of some help as this is where the author usually states his purpose for writing. In the case of revised editions, the reasons for revision and points of difference between revised and earlier editions should be discussed and noted.

The most informative prefatory section is the table of contents. This gives a general framework of the content and reveals the author's method and sequence of development of his subject. Subheadings in the table of contents make more detailed previewing of the material possible. An intelligent use of the contents table enables the pupil to eliminate the unnecessary and irrelevant and to pinpoint the particular areas of study most suitable for his purposes at any one time. For specific details within any such area, the subject index is extremely useful, as here is listed, in alphabetical order, all the supporting data and detailed information on which the main framework of the book is built. The index is particularly valuable for cross referencing when looking for related topics. For following up a topic

E

in depth, guides to further reading and additional resources are frequently provided in the appendix.

Essential attitudes towards textbooks and further reading
Whether using the textbook itself or material complementary to it, a certain ruthlessness on the part of the reader is required. This is essential in order to counteract a widespread attitude towards books which can only be described as religious. Over the centuries the printed word has, for many people, assumed almost supernatural qualities. This no doubt stems from the fact that our earliest books had an almost exclusively religious content, and in addition had such a scarcity value as to render them priceless. Even today, when books are cheap and plentiful, they are still held in veneration. Merely to have seen a statement in print is, for many, a guarantee of its absolute truth – such is the power of suggestion of the printed word, and hence the need to approach reading always in a questioning, critical way. However, from the point of view of efficient reading, books must be regarded as no more than tools which are to be used in our search for knowledge. We take from them what we need, when we need it. I have noticed a tendency on the part of many students, even in higher education, to overread recommended material when working on assignments. When chapter 6 of a certain text has been suggested as helpful in order to complete a given piece of work, students will persist in reading the whole book first before reading the prescribed chapter in detail. They do this, they say, because they want to see how the particular chapter fits into the book as a whole. They need, they say, clear ideas about what precedes the chapter, and then they must read what comes after to see how the ideas in that chapter are developed. The application of SQ3R procedure could obviate much unnecessary expenditure of time and effort. All that is required is to survey the table of contents in conjunction with the relevant parts of the subject index. Skimming within these areas reveals the relevant areas for reading and then, by reviewing and reciting, the information required will be researched and applied to the assignment in hand.

Practical work on the textbook structure
1 General
The success of instruction in the structure of textbooks could be partly measured by a simple test on the following lines:

Appendix, table of contents, edition, index, preface, title.
Choose the most suitable words or phrases from the above list to complete each of the sentences below:
1 The list of chapters and parts of chapters which form an outline is called the

The   is a collection of additional material at the end of the book.
3 The   is the name of the book or story.
    The   is a short preliminary explanation of the author's reasons for writing the book. Here he usually explains how the work and how the material was got together. In this section he may also name the people or institutions who helped, and he may also recommend the best ways of using the book.
5   is the term used to describe all those copies of the book which were printed in the same form at a certain time.
6 The   is a list, in alphabetical order, of the different subjects mentioned and the page numbers where each reference to these may be found. It is usually found at the end of the book.

2   Practical work on specific textbooks

An important theme of this book is that all teachers are to some extent teachers of reading. If a teacher, whatever his specialism, prescribes for his pupils a certain textbook, surely the teacher ought to explain how that particular text is to be used. That teacher should also give understanding of the structure of his specialist text and relate such understanding to the particular course of study which his pupils are following. They should have every help in familiarizing themselves with all the means of instruction and, if the textbook is an important means, it is the subject teacher's responsibility to develop the ability of his pupils to make proper use of it. A useful practical assignment designed to familiarize pupils with specific textbooks would be for each subject specialist to set a questionnaire on the following lines:

Write complete sentences in answer to the following:
1   What is the title of your textbook?
2   What is the author's name?
3   What are the author's qualifications?
4   When was the book published?
6   Who are the publishers?
7   Are any assignments, questions or problems set in the book to help you to study better? If so, describe them.
8   Is the book illustrated? If so, how might the illustrations help you?
9   Are there any charts, maps or diagrams? If so, how may these help you?
10   Where is the table of contents?
11   List the main topics in the contents table.
12   List the subtopics in the contents table.
13   Where is the index?

14 By using the index, state on which pages information about the following may be found (here each subject teacher should provide a list of key words or topics for pupils to reference).
15 Where is the preface?
16 What does the preface tell you?
17 Where is the appendix?
18 What kind of things are in the appendix?
19 How may the appendix help you?
20 Where is the bibliography?
21 How may the bibliography help you?

Part 3

Individualized reading approaches

It is hoped that Part 2 of this book will do much to dispel the common misconception that all reading instruction must necessarily be on a one to one basis. This misconception has arisen from excessive application in junior and secondary schools of approaches such as hearing children read which are more properly relevant to the beginning stage. The insistence in Part 2 on group methods stresses the value of discussion and participation – factors which could not be utilized if instruction were to be on an individual basis only. With oral group methods the children learn from each other as much as from the material. The group approaches recommended have an additional value in countering an excessive emphasis on writing activities in schools. The question is, however, not whether group methods are preferable to individual methods but rather which aspects of a child's reading development can best be furthered by working with others, and which can best be catered for by letting him work on his own. There is an important place for individual reading instruction in junior, middle and secondary schools, though it will be quite different from that considered suitable at the infant stage. There are two major areas in reading extension which call for individual treatment. These are concerned with the acquisition of skills and attitudes, topics which are treated separately in chapters 6 and 7 respectively. Chapter 8 is something of an odd man out in a book otherwise directed at extension level. It acknowledges the fact that some children have gross difficulty in beginning to read and only reach the stage where a start can be made at ages far beyond the infant school period. Such children must be helped individually, and this chapter describes a simple but effective technique which should prove helpful even to the nonspecialist reading teacher.

Chapter 6

Individualized reading development - laboratory/ workshop approaches

Each individual is a composite of his own unique experience. He has his own peculiar needs, abilities, strengths, weaknesses and interests in reading as in any other aspect of human behaviour. He constantly needs to acquire new skills and to sharpen existing skills by practice and by opportunities to apply them to new situations. Because he is unique, both by endowment and by environmental influences, his needs at any one time will rarely be precisely the same as those of another. He will differ from others also in the time he needs to absorb new learning and to perfect it by practice and application Recognition of individual differences in ability, interests and learning rate has led in British primary schools to a widespread disaffection with class methods and to some reduction in average class size, though rarely, except in a few private or special schools, has the reduction been sufficient to make individual teaching possible. Past attempts to individualize teaching have been bedevilled by the absence of suitable materials sufficiently sophisticated to occupy gainfully say thirty-nine different children while the teacher devotes some personal attention to the fortieth.

Fortunately, in the last few years, multilevel apparatus has begun to filter into our schools. First in the market were the SRA *Reading Laboratories*. When the latter were introduced into our schools their defects, which were as obvious as their strengths, deterred many teachers from giving them a trial. At first sight the laboratories did appear somewhat clinical. They were quite unsuitable for nonreaders. They were far too self-contained and lacked built-in devices for directing pupils to using books in a wide ranging way; in fact, the only referencing skills taught were dictionary skills. The materials were separate cards, not books, and teachers felt that the main goal should be the reading of books, not miniature *Reader's Digest* type articles, however interesting they might be. Neither were there opportunities for oral reading or discussion. On this latter point teachers were unnecessarily hard on SRA and were obviously looking for some universal panacea for all-round reading development which

SRA does not claim to provide. Probably the most off-putting elements were the Americanized content and spelling, especially the latter. Even so, many teachers found that the advantages of the earliest imports far outweighed their disadvantages. The pupils found the materials challenging and stimulating. When used on the booster principle, i.e. for one term only in each school year, they provided a focus for reading instruction which the schools had long lacked. When the booster term was over other materials were used to extend the reading horizons of the children. However, those teachers who were critical of the earliest SRA materials can be assured that many of the apparent defects are being put right. The introduction of the Pilot Libraries facilitates and encourages transfer of skills and interests to wider reading, and the library charts with their additional suggestions for further recommended reading direct the children to the wider range of services provided by school and community libraries. Anglicization of content, language usage and spelling is proceeding and the most popular reading laboratory, the IIA, aimed at the top of the junior school, has already been 'internationalized'. SRA *Reading Laboratories* are already in use in nearly 30 per cent of primary schools and some 25 per cent of secondary schools in the United Kingdom.

It was inevitable that with SRA selling well, despite the apparent drawbacks mentioned above, competition from an indigenous product would not be long in coming. This arrived in the form of the Ward Lock Educational *Reading Workshops*. The authors, directing their material at British schools, had obvious advantages over SRA from the point of view of content, language and spelling. Donald and Louisa Moyle (1971) feel that:

> *Reading Workshop* scores on its reading content but lacks a clear view of the development of reading skills. Weight has obviously been placed on the selection and writing of the literature. The questions seem to have been added afterwards. In the SRA *Reading Laboratories*, though the content of the questions is related to the literature, the type and structure of the questioning has been predetermined by an analysis of the growth of reading skills.

My own observations of SRA *Reading Laboratories* and Ward Lock Educational *Reading Workshops* entirely agree with those of Donald and Louise Moyle. The reasons for the differences between the two approaches are not hard to find. SRA is an American import. Its designers wrote for American schoolchildren taught by American teaching methods, which to most British observers are notoriously 'systematic'. It is common for teachers' manuals of American reading schemes to be so comprehensive in their directions and suggestions that they are a great deal thicker than the pupils' texts. British educators when appraising American reading manuals are commonly aghast at the sheer weight of suggestions given and infer that the role of the teacher is relegated to that of a mere instructor and that possibilities for spontaneity and teacher initiative are not considered. On the other hand, the manuals of British reading schemes are rarely more than the thinnest of pamphlets. British teachers are accustomed to using their own initiative in adapting and modifying reading materials and handling them in a variety of ways. In the USA the accent is on structure and systematic programming of skills. In Britain we tend to work from interest and imaginative and creative teaching approaches stemming from it. Thus the SRA *Reading Laboratories* and Ward Lock Educational *Reading Workshops* reflect the teaching attitudes of their respective countries of origin.

In the absence of any large-scale compartive research into the two approaches it is impossible as yet to give anything more than the most subjective opinions, and the only criteria by which teachers can decide which to use are those of structure (SRA) or content (Ward Lock Educational), or, if cost has to be considered, Ward Lock Educational is very much the cheaper, although this is open to discussion. Some teachers point out that with SRA they get a lot more for their money. The teachers' manuals are certainly superior to those provided by Ward Lock Educational, as are the pupils' record books. SRA also provide for listening skills, a field which Ward Lock Educational ignores. Most observers agree that the Ward Lock Educational teachers' manuals would benefit from a thorough revision which would enable teachers to crossreference more easily the reading skills developed through the different levels, even though this might increase the cost factor. Despite this assertion, all the class teachers involved in Dr Alan Little's 1971–2 study for the ILEA of the Ward Lock Educational *Reading Workshops, Language Master* and the *Audio Page* felt that 'they needed no extra assistance other than the teachers' manual when using the Workshop'. The Ward Lock Educational pupils' workbooks, however, are almost universally commended. They are much cheaper than the SRA counterparts and have a simple format, a particularly useful feature of which is that the centre pages, in which the child's progress is recorded by graphs, can be removed for teacher's records when the workbook is full. Another advantage of the Ward Lock Educational workbooks is that they are not copyrighted and teachers are, in fact, encouraged to produce their own. SRA on the the other hand consider their pupils' record books indispensible if the children are to benefit from laboratory type work. Copyright ensures that duplicating and other forms of copying are discouraged. This is a pity. It denies to many schools the benefits of multilevel learning because of the high operating costs of the essential but expendable pupils' materials. A number of observers have commented that they find the SRA record books unnecessarily elaborate. Some simplifications of layout and a resultant reduction in cost would be welcomed by the schools. Ward Lock Educational *Reading Workshops* have nothing corresponding to the Listening Builders provided by SRA in their more advanced laboratories. It may be that this is a wise omission for the treatment of listening skills is not the best feature of SRA. As they are generally taught on whole class lines the individualized approach, which characterizes other elements of SRA, is missing here. Finally a word about phonics. The treatment given by Ward Lock Educational is adequate. The phonic work presented in the SRA Power Builders is oppressively overdone, especially that provided in the laboratories aimed at competent readers in upper junior classes and the lower forms of secondary schools. Children in these age groups who need phonic help could probably get it more enjoyably and in a sequence no less carefully structured by means of Stott's (1962) *Programmed Reading Kit.*

These comments have been made in order to point out that 'cheaper' need not necessarily mean 'worse', but may in fact only mean 'different'. Ward Lock Educational *Reading Workshops* have proved their popularity in British schools in a very short space of time. Over 8,000 *Workshops* have already been sold, 3,000 6–10 *Workshops* and 5,000 9–13 *Workshops.* Some of the differences between the SRA and Ward Lock Educational approaches have been highlighted above. The rest of this chapter will be largely devoted to demonstrating their similarities.

It is a basic premise of this book that laboratory and workshop materials are an essential ingredient in reading instruction. If the teaching of reading is to develop with the sophistication it requires, a considerable variety of approaches and techniques is called for. Group methods need to alternate with individual work, oral work with writing, silent reading with oral reading, and reading for information with reading for pleasure. At one time the teacher may need to operate at a level of basic skill development with one group, at critical reading with another. Other groups may need speeding up while still others may wish to discuss their reading interests in somewhat dilettante fashion. All of these aspects of the teaching of reading are desirable, indeed necessary, and in order to accomplish them the teacher and the groups or individuals with whom she is working at any one time must be guaranteed both the time and the freedom from distraction required to do the job well. The SRA and Ward Lock Educational materials are so designed that each child in the class can work at his own level and at his own pace for quite long periods of time. When the majority of the children are so occupied, the teacher is free to work with the rest at either group or individual level. Without such materials the daily reading lesson, essential for the exploitation of the variety of teaching techniques recommended here, would not be possible. Without a daily reading lesson, during which regular and systematic instruction can be given, reading will continue to have the low status vis-à-vis the more favoured subjects in the timetable, and the grossly inadequate, unstructured and incidental treatment which it currently receives will be perpetuated. It is hoped that the impression has not been given that the SRA *Reading Laboratories* and the Ward Lock Educational *Reading Workshops* are to be considered mere time fillers, thanks to which other and more valuable teaching activities can be undertaken more freely. The laboratories and workshops have their own intrinsic value in providing a structure of skills to be learned, practised, revised and applied plus a range of reading topics which can lead to the acquisition of new interests or supplement or extend interests already acquired. Their particular merit is that the opportunities for reading development are so organized that the pupil may break into the sequence at the point where he personally needs to start, and can go on from there at his own individual pace as far and as fast as his abilities and interests permit.

Multilevel reading schemes – basic assumptions
Implicit in the construction of multilevel reading schemes such as those produced by SRA and Ward Lock Educational are the following assumptions:

1 The pupil should start at his own individual level and work at the skills and concepts appropriate to that level at his own rate.
2 The material should be broken down into very small learning steps. Mastery at each stage leads to progress along a learning gradient of gradually increasing difficulty. The child is constantly motivated to seek and attain progressively higher levels.
3 The responsibility for systematically recording and evaluating progress should be placed on the pupil himself. The motivational value of such responsibility is unquestionable, as is the encouragement which the child is given to compete with his own personal achievement rather than with other children.
4 In order to achieve the sort of pupil responsibility described above the procedures have to be largely self-administrative and within the child's organizational capacity. For this purpose a highly structured pupil's record or workbook is essential. In it all work is written, dated, marked, corrected, recorded and evaluated.
5 Pupils learn from their mistakes, provided that they are corrected as soon as possible after they have been made and detected. Thus a card is marked by the child himself using an answer key as soon as the exercise is completed. The child is trained to substitute correct responses in place of errors, but only after he has deduced the reasons for his errors and for the aptness of the model answers.
6 To ensure growth in vocabulary and comprehension as well as

flexibility of reading rate a great variety of reading matter reflecting a wide range of interests is necessary.

SRA Reading Laboratory and Ward Lock Educational Reading Workshop Components

A typical SRA *Reading Laboratory* consists of a compact box of cards divided into three sections: power builders, rate builders and listening builders. The Ward Lock Educational 9–13 *Reading Workshop* has two main sections, work cards and speed cards, which equate respectively with the power builders and rate builders of SRA.

SRA power builders

These consist of 150 cards divided into ten sets of fifteen cards each. Each set represents a reading level which is designated by a colour. The cards within each set are of equal difficulty. Each card presents a picture and a title designed to stimulate interest in the text. A passage of reading matter follows. The pupils are trained to apply the surveying and questioning strategies of SQ3R to this material. Exercises in comprehension, vocabulary and word study based on the text ensure the application of reading, reviewing and reciting to complete the SQ3R process.

Ward Lock Educational work cards

The 9–13 Workshop consists of 100 cards divided into ten sets of ten cards each. The 6–10 Workshop consists of 150 cards divided into ten sets of fifteen cards each. Each set is colour coded for reading difficulty and the cards within each set are of equal difficulty.

SRA power builders and Ward Lock Educational work cards are designed to develop the following abilities: to understand what is read, to find the main idea and supporting details; to identify the author's main purpose; to increase vocabulary; and to improve spelling.

Each assignment is in three parts. There is a teaching section which introduces and explains new skills followed by a set of directions for applying them. Finally practice material is given on which the newly learned skills can be put to use. There is a separate answer card for each assignment.

SRA rate builders and Ward Lock Educational speed cards

The rate builders consist of 150 cards in ten sets of fifteen, which match the colour levels of the power builders. The Ward Lock Educational 9–13 Workshop provides 100 speed cards in ten sets of ten, matched to the colour levels of the work cards.

On each card is a short passage for reading, followed by a number of comprehension questions. The whole assignment, i.e. reading and answering the questions, has to be completed within a time limit of three minutes. The passages in both power builders/rate builders and work cards/speed cards increase in length and complexity through the different levels. Rate builders and speed cards are designed to increase reading speed, to develop powers of concentration, to encourage rapid understanding of the main ideas and supporting details and ability to think clearly under time pressure. Answer booklets (SRA) and answer cards (Ward Lock Educational) are provided.

SRA listening builders

The teachers' manual contains ten exercises designed to improve the child's ability to listen carefully and to remember what has been heard. Each selection is read aloud by the teacher to the groups or individuals concerned, who then answer a series of questions based on the passage. In the later laboratories, beginning with III B, the listening skills section is augmented by listening and note-taking skills.

Using SRA Reading Laboratories and Ward Lock Educational Reading Workshops in the classroom

Each child is given a reading test. In the case of SRA this is the starting level guide. Ward Lock Educational provide a test card. The results of the test, which are recorded in the pupil's record book or workbook, determine the appropriate starting point. Each reading level is designated by a particular colour. The teacher converts the reading score into a colour score by consulting a chart in the teacher's manual.

It takes four or five sessions to familiarize the children with the organization of the record books and to complete the essential preliminary practice material. After this they start working independently on their individual colour assignments. Thus a child who scores red on the reading test starts work on the red assignments.

When each SRA power builder, rate builder and listening builder, or in the case of Ward Lock Educational, each work card and speed card, have been completed, the child corrects and evaluates his own work, notes and corrects errors, and graphs the results in his record book. With SRA materials, when the graphs show that the child is maintaining a consistently high standard, e.g. 85 per cent or above on four or five consecutive assignments, he is promoted to the next colour level. Children using *Reading Workshops* are expected to work their way through the whole sequence of cards in each set before promotion to the next level. Whichever approach is used, the teacher should inspect the record books periodically and discuss progress with each individual pupil. The children become remarkably adept at interpreting their graph data and assessing their own progress and will themselves provide evidence that they should remain longer at one level or be promoted to the next.

Once the children have started independent laboratory/workshop work, the organization, distribution and collection of materials can safely be entrusted to child monitors. Record books are collected at the end of each session. On the front of each book details of all completed cards are shown. Prior to the next session the monitors, one for each colour group, insert a new assignment plus the relevant answer card at the appropriate colour level into the record books and distribute them to the children in their groups, who immediately begin the new assignments. If, during any one session, promotions are made to higher colour levels, these are recorded on the record books and the monitors concerned distribute appropriate materials for the next assignment. Giving the children responsibility for overall organization of the materials frees the teacher to concentrate entirely on group or individual teaching activity. As she is also freed from the burden of marking she has much more time than the teacher working by traditional methods to make important and varied contributions to reading development.

The laboratories and workshops, by providing the children with challenges always at the right personal level and thus occupying them purposefully for long periods, give great scope for the teacher to exploit a wide range of additional teaching techniques. However, from within the resources of the laboratories themselves stem many opportunities for diagnosis and effective on-the-spot treatment of reading difficulty. For example, in the SRA teacher's handbook is a skills chart which gives a breakdown, card by card, of the sequence and range of skills covered. If a pupil performs badly, say in a certain area of word study, the teacher can take swift and decisive action by giving immediate personalized instruction on the particular skill causing difficulty. Further work and practice on the related cards indicated on the skills chart can then be prescribed until mastery is achieved.

Despite the highly individualized approaches built into the materials there are still opportunities for oral work and discussion. A number of schools have an occasional period known as 'sharing time', during which small groups or individuals give oral reports on current interests and activities. There appears to be no reason why individual pupils, from time to time, should not either summarize or read out the content of the card which they have recently used, so that other children who may be at different colour levels may benefit from material with which they may not otherwise have contact.

Challenging the 'booster' philosophy

It has become generally accepted that the reading laboratory or workshop is best used as a booster, i.e. for intensive work in reading for one school term only in a school year. I personally regard this view as quite outdated. It gained ground in an era when the reading laboratory was almost the sole means available to junior and secondary teachers of developing reading extension in a structured way. Teachers in these categories were generally those who had had the most minimal training in teaching reading and their schools were usually those which gave the least attention to it. Consequently, the philosophy behind the booster principle was 'At least one term in each year let us concentrate on reading. We can then spend the rest of the year doing other things.' However, in recent years, attitudes towards teaching reading have been changing and reading is increasingly seen as a developmental process extending from preschool days well into adulthood. Its importance for adjustment and performance both in school and in adult life has been increasingly recognized. Initial and in-service training in teaching reading has seen considerable extension and in some ATOS courses in teaching reading are compulsory requirements for all those seeking a teaching qualification, whatever their age specialism. Important advances towards teaching the higher order skills have been made and a methodology for extending older children is emerging which is quite different from the set of techniques, approaches and attitudes which characterize instruction at the beginning stage. In view of these facts, the use of laboratories and workshops as boosters only, essential because few other suitable techniques and approaches were available and teacher expertise was minimal, can no longer be recommended as conditions necessitating the application of the booster principle are themselves altering rapidly. The use of the reading laboratory or workshop should be reassessed in the context of an emerging methodology for reading extension. Where once it was the sole medium now it is one of many. Teachers should be considering how it may best function as part of a total battery of extension approaches in which oral work, group work, and individualized teaching which is not laboratory-based may all make significant contributions.

What is advocated here is an extended use of reading laboratories or workshops throughout the period of advanced reading instruction. If reading development is to proceed in an orderly, systematic way, children must have the time to learn new skills, to reinforce the learning, and to apply it as part of their ongoing, all-round development. It would appear quite illogical to concentrate on physical education to considerable depth in just one school term and then to drop it as though it had the plague for the next two. It appears equally illogical to plunge the children into a headlong race in reading development for a single term only in any school year. As children mature physically they apply newly learned skills to the successful accomplishment of tasks which at earlier stages of development would not have been possible. This applies equally to reading growth. Each new skill mastered leads to higher levels of experience and performance which at earlier stages of maturation would have been unattainable. All-round growth, however, requires a certain balance in the range of possible experiences to which the child is exposed. If in the event that teachers were illogical enough to opt for PE in depth in only one school term in three, it would be considered even more illogical to concentrate in that term on leg movements only. It would appear equally illogical to confine reading development to laboratory-type materials for one term and to use the next two to exploit whatever feedback may result.

Reading laboratories and workshops have their undeniable merits, the principal one being that they provide, in a challenging and stimulating way, a sequence and structure for individual reading growth which few teachers could provide from their own resources. It seems unfortunate that children's opportunities to benefit from what multilevel materials have to offer should be restricted to one-third of the school year. It is also bad economics to invest in materials which are not put to maximum use. The availability of the materials should be extended throughout the school year and the children would benefit from the increased time and opportunities for conceptualizing new learning, consolidating new skills and applying them to the whole range of experiences in school.

A daily reading lesson is essential for all children if the varied techniques and approaches required to produce a balanced programme for reading growth are to be applied. If classes were organized on the basis of a daily reading lesson the most central element in such organization would be the reading laboratory or workshop. Each child would benefit from using the materials, say three times a week, throughout the year, though all the children would not be on multilevel work at the same time. Children need not be lonely strivers after knowledge all the time and benefit from working with others on group activities. There must also be time to browse and to read for pure enjoyment. There must also be opportunities to apply reading through writing and other forms of creative expression. In order that these varied aspects of reading may have due attention and may make their different contributions to all-round personal growth, multilevel materials have a central position in any system of organization designed to bring about a comprehensive reading programme. This is so because of the unique contribution that they have to make from the point of view of individual skill development and also because of the freedom they extend to the teacher to exploit a wide range of teaching techniques and the use of other materials and approaches.

Advantages of multilevel reading schemes
The material has very high interest value. The range of interests of the individual laboratories and workshops are extremely well tailored

to the specific age groups for whom they are designed. There is excellent exploitation of those aspects of readability such as vocabulary load, length of words, length and complexity of sentences, which keep the content at the right interest level but allow for variations in reading power. The material is truly multilevel. Exceptional attention is given to individual differences, both from the point of view of progressively graded levels of reading difficulty and of the wide range of topics covered.

From the points of view of practicality and of economy the SRA and Ward Lock Educational materials score highly over traditional approaches. When one considers that so many of the reading needs of up to forty different children can be satisfied by the contents of one single, easily stored, compact box, one can only be full of praise for the ingenuity that has gone into its design and construction. The card material is as durable as most and if lost or damaged, separate components are easily replaceable. The procedures involved in its use are largely self-administrative and ease of overall organization, for which the children can be largely responsible, frees the teacher considerably from the burdens of selecting, collecting, distribution and marking. Freed from such activities, which are always time-consuming and often peripheral, teachers can get down to their central tasks of teaching more effectively and of using time more efficiently. Though the initial cost of a laboratory or workshop, pupils' record books and teacher's handbook may appear high, teachers need to ask themselves how much effective work could be generated for so many different individuals by investing an equivalent amount in other materials. They should also consider the practicality and ease of storage and organization of those materials. Costs per head can, of course, be much reduced by putting the investment to maximum use. Most efficient use of school plant and materials is obtained when activities involving their use are timetabled so that the greatest possible number of classes may use them throughout the day, as in the case of the allocation of the school hall for PE, music, drama, meals, assembly and the like. Daily reading lessons could easily be so timetabled that four different classes could each have uninterrupted and exclusive use of one laboratory or workshop at specified times each day. With average class sizes of thirty-five children, 140 pupils could thus use one common set of materials at remarkably low cost per head.

The SRA and Ward Lock Educational materials provide a focus for improving reading skills in junior, middle and secondary schools. These are the areas in the educational system where reading as a set of skills is often neglected, the assumption being that as the majority of the children can already read, they have no need of definite teaching to improve.

Illustration and presentation are of a high standard and certainly interest and motivate the children. The format makes an interesting contrast with many of the dull, uninspiring, pictureless, traditional attempts to teach comprehension, vocabulary and word study. Each power builder or work card is simply a four-page folder. The children can see that concentrated effort at it for a short period of time will see their assignment completed, then scored, corrected, recorded and evaluated, and all this done by themselves. Such attack is rarely possible with those apparently endless books of comprehension and vocabulary exercises, with questions often unrelated to context and with so many disadvantages from the point of view of feedback. Such exercises often take days for the harassed teacher to mark, and in the interval errors are reinforced by repetition, work is difficult to record and the pupil has no idea of the rate and extent of his progress. In contrast, multilevel materials stretch the child, whether bright, average or dull, by continually motivating him to give his best possible performance and to assume responsibility for recording and evaluating his own personal progress.

Possible drawbacks of multilevel materials
Properly used, laboratories and workshops have remarkably few disadvantages. What criticisms there are stem from improper use of the materials or from the mistaken belief that they constitute a comprehensive programme for all-round reading development. The materials are not a universal panacea for all reading ills nor do they provide avenues leading to instant success in all aspects of reading extension. Teachers must supplement the laboratory/workshop approach with other approaches and materials if a balanced programme is to be achieved.

In general, the sra *Reading Laboratories* and Ward Lock Educational *Reading Workshops* have most to offer in the area of reading efficiency. Built-in opportunities for the application of the sq3r study system, attention to speed and accuracy, and thorough structuring of the stages of skill development give distinct advantages over anything teachers can provide from their own resources to produce better and faster readers. sra and Ward Lock Educational materials are at their weakest in the area of critical reading and in the direct fostering of the habit and enduring love of reading for pleasure. Though some attention is paid to critical reading and there are opportunities for evaluation, a great deal of the comprehension is at a purely literal level and there is a need for much supplementation by teachers with techniques such as the oral discussion activities described in Part 2. In this respect it is a pity that sra is so jealous of copyright as much of the material is ideal, particularly for deletion activities. There is naturally little scope for oral work and discussion in an approach which is so highly individualized. Teachers would do well, therefore, to work outside the sra *Reading Laboratories* and Ward Lock Educa-

F

tional *Reading Workshops* at approaches in which oral discussion and group participation figure prominently.

The proof of the teacher's ability to teach reading well is that he turns out children who not only can read, but do read; readers, that is, who have formed a habit of reading which endures. There is no guarantee that such habits are an automatic endproduct of reading laboratory/workshop approaches. Children who catch the reading habit generally come from literate home backgrounds where books are used, enjoyed and encouraged. Where children lack the home background and conditions which generate the reading habit, their teachers must personalize the conditioning processes required by individual teaching of a kind which multilevel materials cannot supply. The next chapter describes how this can be done.

From my own personal experience I have not found reading laboratories or workshops helpful with teaching severely retarded children. The children with reading ages under 8.0 years, who form the remedial groups in junior and secondary schools, are rarely capable of the sustained, independent work required. I have found other approaches and materials more helpful, and these are described in Chapter 8.

Finally, the development of continuous writing is likely to be severely limited if multilevel work is the sole means of instruction. The majority of the questions are of the multiple choice variety and the child is rarely asked to supply anything more than a letter, e.g. A or B or C or D, to indicate his response, or a single word at most. Such response devices give the material the objectivity without which its many advantages from the point of view of immediate detection and self-correction of errors would not be possible. Obviously the development of continuous writing is not among those particular advantages.

Teachers who are aware of the strengths and weaknesses of multilevel approaches are likely to have realistic expectations of their possibilities and to use them most effectively. Such teachers will use them at the points where they are strong, but will supplement them with a variety of other approaches and materials in a well-balanced programme of reading extension.

Chapter 7

Individual reading interviews

In recent years teachers in junior and secondary schools have had considerable success in getting children to read for information. The explanation for this lies largely in the emphasis given to topic and project-type approaches in the schools. To support these approaches there has been a great expansion of reference sections in class, school and community libraries, and the publishers have responded to the demand by producing a great quantity of factual material which is well illustrated and presented. Now it is important in teaching reading that children should be trained to use books to find information which will expand existing interests and lead to new ones, and that they should have frequent opportunities to apply what they have learned in varied forms of written expression. However, if this is the only form of reading undertaken by children and actively promoted by teachers, the project method has obviously been overdone and has reached proportions which exclude the use of books for other desirable purposes, particularly that of reading for sheer enjoyment. It appears to me that this is the state of reading in many of our schools today. Paradoxically, the greater the success that teachers have had in promoting reading for information, the less time and encouragement there has been for reading in the round. The most minimal of factual reading leads in many of our schools to great quantities of writing, painting, cutting-out, pasting-in, model making, play production and other forms of so-called creative expression. On inspection, a great deal of this 'creative' work turns out to be dull and unoriginal. Much of the writing is mere verbatim transcription and much of the illustration mere tracing or copying. Not only does the vast amount of time and effort devoted to this kind of activity correspondingly reduce the time available for fictional reading, but the sheer volume of production often defies the attempts of conscientious teachers to mark it with any degree of thoroughness. Consequently, great numbers of errors in comprehension, vocabulary, grammatical usage and concept development go undetected and uncorrected and are, in fact, reinforced by frequent repetition. Attempts to keep up with marking leave even less time for an equally important teaching activity, namely the development and elucidation of concepts for which time for discussion of work and interests with groups and individuals is required. When project methods have reached such a stage it is time for teachers to pause and ask themselves what they are really doing and why they are doing it. The current child-centred approaches quite rightly put the responsibility for learning on the child himself and make interest the starting point. However, the teacher has much more to do than to provide the stimuli and the opportunities. She must be much more concerned with the quality of children's learning and with the effectiveness of her own teaching. If the teacher accepts the three-fold goal of reading extension as that of producing critical, efficient and habitual readers, she must control and organize her teaching and the time and resources available to do it so that a balanced programme, in which all these aspects of development receive attention, is put into practice. Chapters 3 to 6 have suggested practical ways in which attention can be given to critical and efficient reading. The purpose of this chapter is to review past and present attitudes and approaches towards developing the life-long love for, and habit of, reading both for information and pleasure, and to describe a technique for developing the reading habit which involves a skilled and personal involvement of teacher with reader.

In education we never seem to be able to move forward on a broad front. At the administrative level we expand our universities at the expense of primary school expansion and modernization. We raise the school leaving age at one end and neglect to provide nursery schools at the other. It is the same with reading. At the beginning stage we have flung out systematic phonic work in favour of all-out look and say teaching. In junior and secondary schools, never strong in reading, we have been in danger of forsaking reading altogether and writing has become the dominant activity, despite the fact that it is the least used of the three RS outside school and in adult life. Nevertheless, the public libraries are well used and new books continue to appear in great profusion. It appears to me, however, that reading tastes and attitudes towards reading have changed considerably over a generation. Where once fiction had the lion's share and reading was done mainly for pleasure, much more reading is now done at a factual level and for a variety of personal and practical purposes. This trend in itself is no mean thing and reflects a well educated general public whose members are capable of adjusting their reading purposes to their own individual needs and interests. A variety of factors – technological, social and economic changes and, of course, the influence of the schools – all contributed to the growth of popular factual reading. Today with shorter working hours and increased leisure, the growing army of 'do it yourself' enthusiasts tackle activities which previously would have been assigned to specialists, assisted by a constant stream of 'do it yourself' literature. Increased leisure and the general increase in spending power have led to large-scale participation in a wide range of interests which a generation ago were confined to a comparative few. Books on how to make, sail, and maintain and improve the performance of boats have a ready sale, as do all sorts of other books ranging from bee-keeping to flower arrangement. Television has made a notable contribution to the growth of reading interests. Through this medium, charming and urbane egyptologists are weekly visitors in the humblest dwellings, have put the tenants under their spell, and have been known to send them in their thousands to the nearest library or bookshop to find out more about an exciting new hobby. Many other specialists, acknowledged leaders in their respective fields, and backed by all the compelling resources of the communications industry, have made their different contributions to a wide range of experience which has generated new reading interests for millions. Now television and the Open University have given opportunities for study and improved qualifications to many thousands. Valuable though such reading growth is, it has been achieved to some extent at the expense of reading material of a more fictional or imaginative kind. All people engaged in practical pursuit of their skills and interests fired by factual reading have correspondingly less time to devote to reading of an imaginative kind. This is not to suggest that one kind of reading is better than another, merely that many kinds of reading are better than just one, and that the more purposes one has for reading, the more reading can contribute to the fullest development of the whole personality.

It may be that times and conditions have so changed over the space of one generation that reading for pleasure will never again have quite the importance that it once had. When I was a very small boy before the days of radio, the talking film and television, I used to read at least one whole book every winter evening. There was nothing else to do. Nowadays technology provides a constant stream of potted entertainment within the home and the family car brings within range a host of easily accessible pleasures beyond it. But however good the film or record, the viewer or listener is never much more than a passive recipient of a succession of fleeting images and impressions. Such impressions are received only once. Further thought depends largely on memory and is therefore often fragmentary or imperfectly retained. With a book the reader is active and controls, rather than is controlled by, the medium. He can vary his pace to suit the material or purpose for which he is reading. He can read ahead or go back, if necessary rereading important parts for later review, analysis or comparison.

However, the purpose of this chapter is not to run down the canned entertainment industry or the reading of factual material. Both have their undoubted merits. The point being made is that if these are the only pleasures and the sole reading fare respectively, the opportunities for full growth and development are likely to be unnecessarily limited, deprived, as they will be, of the whole field of literature which can enrich and extend the range of possible experience. If we deprive children of this, we deprive them of opportunities to share the adventures and ideas of others. In a world in which there is much maladjustment – delinquency, vandalism, drug and bingo addiction, overcrowded prisons – there is certainly need to explore our own personalities and problems and possibly to solve the latter by appreciating and understanding the problems of others. Again, in a society whose complexity demands much regulation and uniformity there is a need to provide opportunities for fun and escape. We need, too, to discover the ethical values which help to form character and to develop worthwhile tastes and interests. In order that all these things may be done a literary diet much more varied than factual reading only must be provided by our schools.

Teachers have not been unaware of the problems mentioned but have in the past usually lacked both the know-how and the time to tackle them effectively. Attempts to promote the reading habit have usually been too vague and generalized to make any real impact on the individual reader. Vague exhortations to read more, to join the library, to try such and such an author, have not had notable success. Nor have remarks on end of term reports such as 'Could read more!', 'Does not read enough!', had much motivational value. Book fairs, exhibitions, readings, reports, book clubs and library visits all have a part to play in generating and maintaining interest in reading, but are generally too spasmodic and unrelated to promote the reading habit if it is not already there. To be really effective the problem must be tackled at an individual level and teachers are generally ill equipped to do this. In the first place some knowledge of children's literature, and especially of the favourite reading interests of one's own particular class, are required. Teachers are not well-known for keeping abreast of children's literature and consequently are ill-equipped to advise or suggest if the only acquaintance they have with it is their recollections of their own schoolday reading. It would be an extremely rare teacher who could say that she has even read all the books in her own class library. And yet such a requirement is a minimal qualification if one is to have the responsibility for selecting reading matter of a sufficiently varied nature to suit the different needs, abilities and interests of an average class. Another essential is to have a detailed knowledge of each child's reading abilities and tastes. Without this the teacher cannot possibly guide reading growth by recommending further work by favourite authors or related material by others.

In these days of speed reading it is no great task to read all the book in one's class. The range of concepts and complexity of ideas and vocabulary in children's literature are rarely so difficult as to tax the reading power of the average teacher. One can easily train oneself on such simple material to use out and out speed reading techniques. The simplest of these is to place a pencil down the centre of each page and to read down the pencil, avoiding any tendency towards left to right eye movements or of going back to clear up certain points. This technique is known as vertical reading and, providing the content is not too difficult, it allows the reader to pick up enough key words and phrases to make sense of the whole without having to read every part. Once the major task of reading the entire class library has been achieved, say at the rate of four or five books a night, it is a comparatively simple matter to keep up with small additions to stock from time to time.

Acquiring a detailed knowledge of pupils' reading interests has been much more difficult. First of all, not all of a child's reading tastes, considered at any one time, are likely to last long; indeed some are likely to be quite ephemeral. To record systematically and to take note of such short term changes as well as to recognize more consistent patterns and preferences has so far baffled the majority of teachers. And it has proved impossible to find the time in which all this is to be done.

Actually, all the problems so far raised can be overcome by the adoption of one simple device known as the individual reading interview. All it involves is that each child records all that he reads on ruled record cards, one for each separate piece of reading matter. Each time a new book is started, the child notes the date on his card. He also puts the date when he finishes the book, regardless of whether he has completed it or not. He also records the chapters referred to and the number of pages read. Finally, the child makes a brief personal comment on the content. Once a term, the teacher takes the child's record cards and teacher and child discuss them together informally. The teacher is thus spared the labour of what could be a most complex piece of recording and yet a detailed pattern of development is constantly available to her for each child in the class. The child reveals in his record the extent and general pattern of his own reading growth and is constantly encouraged to enlarge and enrich it. Time is readily available, given a well organized reading lesson every day (see Chapter 9), to review progress and guide further growth. During reading interviews numerous opportunities occur to explain imperfectly developed concepts and comprehension and vocabulary difficulties can be cleared up as they arise. The insights gained by the teacher into the reading tastes and abilities of the individual pupils can be put to use when selecting additional materials and can be a considerable help when planning and organizing current and future learning experiences for the children. The child himself benefits by developing insights into his own performance and potential as a reader and over a period of time he gradually builds up a realistic self-picture. Awareness of his own strengths and weaknesses, likes and dislikes, is essential to the formation of his reading habits and tastes as well as to the development of his whole character and personality.

Recently I have been able to conduct a reading programme for a class of third year juniors for a whole year. Each child began his reading record at the start of the year and had an individual reading interview with me towards the end of each term. I was thus able to build up a good picture of each child's reading development and to give here and there an extra prod or stimulus to read more by following up an interest by filtering in appropriate material. John, a ten year old of exceptional prowess, never failed to surprise me with the catholicity of his tastes and the many purposes which he found for reading of different kinds. His third interview, which was recorded, is reproduced below in order that teachers may consider for themselves the benefits that both teacher and child may derive from such an experience. I must add that few interviews would be as lengthy as this one. The boy in question had covered a great deal of ground in the term. The knowledge that he was to have such an interview was in itself an incentive to do this. He was obviously enjoying the experience of discussing books with a fellow dilettante and was thus accorded whatever time was needed so that our discussion was characterized by mutual pleasure and devoid of any hint of rush or strain. All work in teaching reading should have these characteristics, both for teacher and child.

T   Hello, John. It seems a long time since we had a good look at your reading record so let's see what's on it. Now there's the *World Football Handbook*. This seems to be the latest. What have you got down about this? 1972, written by Brian Glanville. How did you find this one?

J   I got it from school in the Chip Club.

T   I see. How much did this cost you?

J   25 pence.

T   Anything particularly good about it?

J   Well it's compact.

T   Yes?

J   And it's got all the facts you want to know at a glance.

T   I see. What sort of facts did you want at a glance?

J   Well, I had the *1970 Football Handbook* and it hadn't got the latest ones in, you know the up-to-date ones. So I thought I might as well get right up-to-date with this one.

T   I see. Is there much about European football in this one?

J   Yes, there's a lot.

T   So it's been worth the money then, and you're enjoying this still?

J   Yes, very much.

T Very good. Now, I see that we've got Showell Styles once again. What about this one? This is *Wolf Cub Island*.

J Yes. Well it starts off as a letter to a boy called Gary Preston. It's about a bird called the roseate tern and it finishes off with three robbers who have stolen some goods and hidden them in a cave on a rock called Wolf Rock and Gary eventually stops them by setting a watch on it and calling the police by means of signal torches.

T It sounds very good. You've read this before though, haven't you? This is the second time you've read this one.

J Yes, it is.

T Well, you read it last term, and you've read it again, so it must be good.

J Yes, it's a very good book.

T And it's not the first time you've read Showell Styles, is it?

J There are two other books I've read by him—that's *Cubs in the Castle*, this book.

T That's *Wolf Cub Island*?

J Yes, and there's another one called *The Sea Cub*.

T You're not in the cubs, are you John?

J No.

T No, but you enjoy reading these particular books about them?

J Yes.

T Very good. And no doubt you'll probably read it again next term, will you?

J Well, I hope so.

T Good! Now what on earth is this one here called *Snoopy*?

J It's a comic strip book about a dog called Snoopy.

T I see. It sounds a bit like Charlie Brown.

J It's got Charlie Brown in it. Snoopy is Charlie Brown's dog.

T I thought there was something familiar about it. However, as it's a comic strip book we'll relegate that to the second division for now, shall we? Now this is an interesting thing on your card— *Hugo's Spanish Simplified*. What's that one all about?

J It's for teaching you Spanish.

T Yes, I thought it was, but what's the purpose of that?

J I'm going abroad to Majorca for the holidays with my father.

T Well, you are lucky. Do you find it hard to learn Spanish from a book like this?

J No, not really. Not after a bit of practice.

T I see. And what sort of things have you been doing with the book?

J I've just been learning some phrases and doing the first lesson.

T Indeed! Now what phrases do you know?

J Well, the ones I know off by heart are 'buenos dias', 'buenos tardes', and 'buenos noces', which mean in order, 'good day', 'good afternoon' and 'good night'.

T Very good! Well, I hope you have a good time in Majorca and I hope you get a chance to use your Spanish. It's very good, that, to try to learn Spanish at ten, all on your own. Does your daddy speak Spanish?

J A bit.

T Does your mummy?

J I don't think so.

T No? So this is your idea really, this. Very good. Now, here's an old friend, eh? *Paddington Helps Out*, Michael Bond. You had this on your card last time.

J Yes, and I probably had it on the term before.

T I'm sure you did. Is Michael Bond your favourite author?

J Well, for certain books.

T What kind of books would you say he's your favourite for?

J Paddington.

T The Paddington books! Has he written any others?

J He's written nine others: *Paddington Helps Out*, er, let me see ...

T Well, you've got one on a card here—*Paddington Takes the Air*. Have you read them all?

J I've not read two.

T Which are they?

J *Paddington Goes to Work*, and *Paddington Goes to Town*.

T I see. *Paddington Helps Out*? Sounds as though there may be some unfortunate happenings here, because he's too helpful, isn't he?

J Yes.

T Is this the one where he helps with the decorating?

J No. This is the one where Mr and Mrs Brown are ill and he has to cook the dinner and look after the house.

T Oh! Poor Mr and Mrs Brown! And *Paddington Takes the Air*? Is he flying then, in this one?

J No, and he doesn't go on the wireless either.

T No? He's not going on the air?

J Well, he does go on TV.

T Does he? That's probably where the title comes from then. Anything particularly exciting in this one?

J Yes, the case of the doubtful dummy.

T The case of the doubtful dummy? I see, he's turning detective, is he?

J Yes.

T That sounds as though it might be mysterious. How does he come to do this?

J Well, he reads a lot of Carlton Dale detective stories and he writes a letter to Carlton Dale and he goes out on a foggy night to post it. The only trouble is, he doesn't know Carlton Dale's address. But he feels sure the post office will know it as he once solved a case for them called the case of the missing mailbags.

T It sounds very good. And you've read that one before, haven't you?

J Yes, it was earlier on this term.

T Yes. So that's twice in one term you've read the same book, so it must be good. In fact, you've read nearly all the Paddington ones, as you say. Which of them would you recommend most to the children who haven't read Paddington yet?

J The first three.

T The first three he wrote. And the first one he wrote was just *Paddington*, wasn't it? Is that rght?

J Yes—*A Bear Called Paddington.*

T *A Bear Called Paddington*! Yes. that's right. Now this looks a very difficult one for you—*David Copperfield.*

J Well, I don't find it difficult.

T You don't? Was it a thick book or not?

J Not very thick.

T I see. Which edition was it?

J It's the ...

T Was it a paperback?

J Yes, it is.

T I see. Was it the one which had a picture from the film on the front?

J Yes, that's the one.

T I see. So it's the book of the film really. It's not the full length one. Have you seen the film?

J Yes, I have.

T And did you enoy the film as much as the book?

J Yes. I think the film wasn't as good as the book in the descriptions.

T No. Well, there aren't any descriptions in the films, are there? You just see them. You have to describe things in a book because you can't actually see them. So you have to imagine it.

J There's a better general description in the book, you know. . . .

T Oh yes! It's a very good book. I would have thought it was a bit hard for you, for a ten year old.

J Well, I don't find it difficult.

T No? Good. Is there anyone you particularly liked in the book?

J David.

T Yes. You'd like David. Anyone whom you particularly disliked?

J Mr Nell, the headmaster at the school.

T Oh, yes! He wasn't a very nice person, was he? Not as nice as your headmaster here, was he?

J No.

T No. And I see this sounds like another book of the film, because this is *2001, A Space Odyssey*. I notice you haven't finished reading that, you've only read ninety-odd pages.

J   A hundred and nine.

T   Sorry, a hundred and nine pages of this one. Have you seen the film?

J   Yes, I have.

T   Recently?

J   Yes it was about a month ago.

T   I see. And you got the book because you enjoyed the film.

J   Yes.

T   And in this case is the book better than the film? Say, like *David Copperfield* was?

J   No, it's not as good as the film.

T   Not as exciting. And in any case I think it's a rather hard book this one, isn't it?

J   Well, I suppose it is.

T   Yes. You'd rather have the film. OK. Well, it's nice to see you reading hard books like this, and still you're enjoying it because you're determined to finish it, aren't you?

J   Definitely.

T   Now there's this old friend of yours *The Schoolboy's Annual* cropping up once again. You read this all the time.

J   Yes, I do.

T   Because you put it down on your card each term.

J   I do.

T   Now then. What sort of things do you keep turning to in this one? This is the one you got for Christmas last, isn't it?

J   I keep turning to those thriller stories, like war, and aircraft and swimming.

T   Yes, you're a good swimmer aren't you. And there are a lot of aircraft in this one. I've not seen it on your cards but I seem to remember very recently that you were reading one about aircraft.

J   Yes, it's *Do You Know About Aircraft*?

T   Perhaps it was last term that, or was it the term before?

J   No, it was last term.

T   Yes I know it was recently because you were doing some work in class on it, weren't you?

J   Yes I was.

T   Is this an *Observer* book?

J   No. It's a *Collins Paygant (sic) of Knowledge*.

T   Collins ... ?

J   Paygant of Knowledge.

T   Pageant! Pageant of Knowledge.

J   Pageant.

T Yes, Pageant! What's a pageant?

J Er. . . .

T Well, a pageant is a sort of display. And in this book all the different aircraft are displayed as if it were a 'pageant' of figures in history, except that they're aircraft being displayed and described for you.

J In history, going up.

T Yes. It's exactly that—in an exhibition or a show. That's what pageant means. So I've no doubt you'll keep on reading your *Schoolboy's Annual* until you get your next edition, won't you? Now, another old favourite of yours you're reading again this term and that's *Blue Peter*.

J Yes, that's the seventh book.

T *The Seventh Book of Blue Peter*. Do you have all the other six by the way?

J No. This is the only one.

T The only Blue Peter one you've got. But this is the most recent one isn't it?

J No. This was last year's. There is an eighth.

T Is there a number eight? I see. You've not managed to get that one from anywhere.

J No, not yet.

T What's the best thing in *Blue Peter*, if anyone wanted to read it?

J The nonfiction stories.

T The nonfiction. Yes, because they're always going out seeing something exciting, aren't they?

J Like Henry the Eighth.

T You mean the television serial?

J It's something to do with that. It's how they get the stages and how they get the clothes done for the whole thing.

T Did you see it on television, any of this Henry the Eighth?

J I saw one episode.

T You saw one. I see. This is the one where we had trouble last term over the word 'scribe' wasn't it? There was the article on 'The Queen's Scribe' and you thought a scribe was a thing.

J Yes.

T Something that she owned.

J Yes.

T Can you remember now what the scribe was, or who the scribe was?

J It's a person who writes the queen's letters to important people.

T I see. So when they make me Lord Walker he'll write to me, will he?

J I suppose so.

T Yes, but a scribe is a man isn't he? In the bible there were the

Scribes and Pharisees. Who were the Scribes? Can you remember me telling you this?

J   I don't think I can.

T   You've forgotten? Well I'll tell you again. In those days very few people could write, so if they wanted to send a letter to someone . . .

J   . . . they had to . . . it's like in an office . . . where the men tell the girls what they want writing down. . . .

T   Yes, in a way. Except the men can write today and in those days they couldn't and so they had to pay somebody else to write for them. Well now, that's quite a good term's reading and I'm sure there's quite a lot of other stuff that you've not got in your record. You take comics, don't you?

J   Yes, a lot of comics.

T   Which one do you take regularly?

J   *Scorcher and Score*—it's a football comic.

T   *Scorcher and Score*? Not *Score and Roar*?

J   Well, it used to be *Score and Roar,* but *Scorcher* and *Score and Roar* combined to give *Scorcher and Score.*

T   I see. I thought it sounded vaguely familiar. And this is all football, isn't it?

J   Yes, all football.

T   Very good. Well, I hope to see you next term and to see a lot more books on your record. Well done! And keep it up! Thank you John.

J   Thank you, Mr Walker.

An analysis of this reading interview reveals many points of interest to the reading teacher. Obviously, it was not designed in this particular case to prod a reluctant reader into further reading. The boy concerned was more than competent for his age and was obviously accustomed to using books for a variety of purposes, and so this interview took more the form of a review. Even so, it is noticable that with each term more reading had been done and it is possible that the expectation of a reading interview may have contributed in some degree to such extension. It was possible to clear up one or two vocabulary and pronunciation difficulties such as scribe and pageant, and in the case of the word scribe to revise a concept which had been tackled previously but had obviously been forgotten. It was particularly interesting to observe that the boy was in the early stages of conceptualizing the rival abilities of two different art forms, i.e. the film and the book, to handle a common theme. Because of the child's immaturity and the complexity of the range of concepts involved, it was not thought worthwhile to develop this to any depth. However, a mental note was made that on a future occasion it could be profitable to initiate discussion with some of the brighter children on the rival merits of different art forms.

It is obvious that the main beneficiary of this particular interview was the teacher. He was able to find out in a very short time a great deal about the child concerned both as a reader and person, and to add this to information previously acquired in a similar manner. He was reminded that films have a powerful role in stimulating children's reading. In John's case his reading of *David Copperfield* and *2001, A Space Odyssey* was inspired by his having first seen the films. Television, the teacher was reminded, has a similar role. For children in the junior school, programmes such as *Blue Peter* obviously have great appeal and more direct classroom discussion of good current programmes could probably lead to a widening of reading interests for many children. The capacity of children to get continuing pleasure from reading and rereading established favourites was also noted. Showell Styles and Michael Bond had given much pleasure to this boy. As John was one of the acknowledged class leaders and his power to influence the reading tastes of others in sharing time (see Chapter 9) was considerable, I decided to requisition the full range of Showell Styles's and Michael Bond's works for the class library.

Without some device such as the reading interview it is impossible to acquire at grassroots level a working knowledge and understanding of what the children are reading. The only way to find out what the children do read is to ask them and keep on asking. This is often most important from the point of view of keeping up with changes of title, new editions and the like. For example, I was not aware that there were in fact eight *Blue Peter* annuals, that the first Paddington book was *A Bear Called Paddington* and that the popular boys' weekly *Score and Roar* had amalgamated with *Scorcher*. My false assumptions on these points were politely corrected by John, who thereby increased his self-esteem by opportunities to teach his teacher, who was himself grateful for such information and the chance to bring his working knowledge more up-to-date. At the same time I was able to add considerably to my knowledge of John as a person and not merely as a reader. Thus his recently acquired custom of wearing a cap on every possible occasion was explained by identification with his fictional hero Paddington, whose hat was an inseparable piece of apparel. Football and swimming were emerging as enduring interests and much reading was linked to these sports. John had recently been promoted to regular goalkeeper for the first school soccer eleven, had just won his bronze medal at swimming and was now preparing for his silver. These interests, which were shared by the majority of boys of his age group, made me determined to strengthen the sports section of the class reference library by including more straightforward coaching manuals, particularly for association football and swimming.

Given a certain flexibility in tailoring the form of the interview to the needs of different pupils, it is possible to give help and encouragement to all the individual members of the class. Because the interview is personalized and timetabled (i.e. at fairly regular intervals) it has more impact on the individual than the more generalized approaches which the majority of teachers use. The generalized approaches would themselves have greater impact if the insights developed in reading interviews were applied when supporting activities were being planned. To work at such a personally involved level, time and freedom from distraction are essential, and it would seem impossible to implement so individualized an approach without the ability to build in the necessary supporting conditions. Only a regular daily reading lesson can provide the organizational framework within which the necessary interrelationships between group and individual work can be established and maintained. One needs also to organize for the development of critical reading skills, for constantly increasing efficiency in reading, and for the interaction of these factors with the furthering of the habit of reading. In Chapter 9 practical organizational procedures for promoting all-round reading growth are described in detail.

In a modern educational system, with the accent more and more on individual and small group activity and away from whole class teaching, teachers are becoming increasingly conscious that the more they know about the child in every way, the more they are able to help him from day to day in the classroom by organizing work based on his interests and adapted to his ability and speed of working. The reading interview has a great deal to offer in building up over the whole period of junior, middle and secondary school, a continuing profile of the growing child. A cumulative record, provided in simple form by the child himself, and passed on from teacher to teacher with each new year of schooling, could provide such a profile with the minimum of administrative fuss and bother. I, personally, would like to see a much greater extension of such information-gathering devices allied with much more parental involvement with the day to day processes of education. Child, parents and teacher working together can do more for the individual pupil than by working in isolation. I would like to see, for example, a number of schools experimenting with reading interviews to which the parents were also invited. The possibilities for reading growth and extension of such a partnership are considerable and are crying out for exploitation and evaluation by teachers and researchers.

Finally, in order to put to the most effective use the insights into individual reading tastes and interests gained from reading interviews, teachers must be prepared to seek more precise methods and instruments for measuring readability. When the teacher has to recommend reading matter for developing readers she has to be sure not only that the content has the correct interest value, but also that the pupil will be able to read it without undue difficulty. Nothing puts children off reading more than material which is too difficult. Therefore, the teacher has to be sure that the vocabulary, concepts, ideas and complexity of sentences used are related to the child's ability to understand them. In the past, teachers have been prone to using hit and miss methods, based on opinion and subjective experience, rather than on objective measures. Though a great deal has yet to be done in the field of readability measurement, in the short term we have to rely on what scientific measures we have, imperfect though they are. The use of a device such as Fry's Readability Graph, plus the insights gained from subjective experience and observation, could lead to a simple system of classification of books by readability levels. Each reading level could be designated by a particular colour and an appropriate coloured sticker attached to the front or spine of each book. In this way the teacher could guard against boring the better readers by suggesting material which is too simple, or against frustrating the dull by offering material which is far too hard.

Chapter 8

Remedial reading

According to the Kent survey of 1966 (Morris 1966) some 25 per cent of children entering junior school require a continuation of the sort of teaching associated with the infant school and have still not got through the earlier stages of beginning reading. Since 1966 there has been no evidence of a substantial improvement in national reading standards and as Kent is a representative county one can assume that about a quarter of the children of England and Wales are still struggling with reading in their first junior year. The general reaction of junior teachers responsible for handling these children has been, for a long time, to ask 'What have the infant teachers been doing?' The implications behind the question are that:

1 Infant teachers have failed in their job.
2 Teaching beginning reading is not a job for the junior teacher.

Are the infant schools letting us down? Certainly some improvement in basic reading could be achieved if some infant schools adopted more systematic approaches, relied less heavily on exclusively look and say approaches, started phonic work earlier and continued it for longer, and gave children some confidence and independence in attacking new words. Experimental forms of organization such as vertical grouping which appear to be aimed at socialization rather than at academic achievement certainly pose problems, especially for systematic recording of reading progress. There are extreme forms of child-centredness which result in very small children having apparently unwarranted freedom to choose activities in which they may or may not engage. There is also in some schools an excessive amount of time and attention devoted to creative activities of a nonlinguistic kind. Many of these developments result from the way in which infant teachers are trained. The persons specifically responsible for this in the past have tended to have qualifications in child development and to be concerned with the all-round development of children rather than with rigorous attention to the skills and attitudes essential to teaching reading. However, over the last five years there is evidence of a much greater commitment in the colleges to the teaching of reading and of increasingly specialist approaches to it. Despite what has been said, infant schools can take considerable credit for achieving a success rate as high as 75 per cent. In view of the wide range of individual differences and the heavy load of content in the successive stages of beginning reading, it is patently asking too much of our infant schools to cover all the ground with all the children in their first two to three years in school. A great deal of time is spent at the early infant stage in dealing with various aspects of socialization and in giving children the oral language background which is vital to reading success. Infant teachers could be spared much of this activity given more generous nursery school provision. An extension of schooling at the nursery end would make available to teachers a longer period for observation and assessment of children, and could lead to earlier identification of, and more suitable treatment for, those who are at risk as potential nonreaders. Infant schools are also notoriously handicapped in having to deal with oversized classes on undersized requisition and library allowances.

Given these factors, it seems reasonable to expect the junior school to take some responsibility for early reading teaching, consolidating early skills for the majority and being prepared to make a formal beginning with those whose rate of maturation is slower than the normal. It is almost incredible that a high proportion of those 25 per cent of children entering the junior school not reading should, after a further eight years of schooling, go out into adult life functionally illiterate. Junior teachers have a clear responsibility for teaching beginning reading. The fact that historically this responsibility has not been accepted reflects great shortsightedness and impracticality on the part of the training institutions. The reading needs of the junior school have had minimal treatment in initial training courses. Though there is evidence, again over the last five years, of increasing provision for the junior trainee in college, there has been lacking a clear set of goals for reading at junior school level and a relevant methodological framework by which realistic aims might be achieved. Expertise in teaching beginning reading has been acquired by many a junior teacher only after a long and painful process during which there have been many casualties both among teachers and taught. Junior schools have also been remarkably slow to adopt the sort of organizational measures recommended by Morris in 1966. One suggestion was to staff the first junior class either with teachers trained in infant methods or with teachers with infant school experience. Obviously, given the right personnel, what is then needed is a reading drive on the part of schools to equip the staff with the time, conditions and resources to break the back of the reading problem at as early a stage as possible. There is little evidence of such a reading drive in many of our junior schools and it seems to me that where this is lacking the presence of infant staff using infant methods offers no guarantee of success. If infant methods have failed the child for his first two to three years in school there is obviously little point in persisting with similar methods in the junior school. The child who has failed with traditional approaches in the infant school has, over two to three years, almost certainly built up a resistance to books and a thoroughly negative attitude towards them. As the commonest method of teaching beginning reading is to hear the child read his way through the successive stages of a commercially produced reading scheme, it makes little sense to give further opportunities for failure to the already failed reader by continuing the practice in the first junior year.

What is certain is that whatever needs doing needs to be done before the child finishes his first year in the junior school. The farther the child moves away from the infant period, the greater are his chances of failing in reading altogether. With each successive junior year he comes increasingly in contact with both teachers and peers for whom beginning reading is no major concern. If he has not made a reasonable start sometime during the junior school period his chances of ever achieving literacy are remote. The secondary school is no place in which to begin to learn to read. It seems a reasonable reaction when faced with nonreaders for secondary teachers to hold up their hands in horror and ask what primary teachers have been doing over a period of at least six years. And it is about the only reaction of which the majority of secondary teachers are capable. If the initial training of junior personnel to teach reading has until recently been suspect, that accorded to secondary trainees has been nonexistent. This reflects an ostrich-like attitude on the part of the training establishments which borders on the criminal. Despite the undoubted presence of large numbers of illiterate and semiliterate children in our nonselective secondary schools, the colleges and universities have persisted in turning out highly trained subject specialists who, though all dependent on the ability of their pupils to read, have had little or no training in developing that ability where it is lacking. Worse, the system of organization in the majority of secondary schools, dependent on rigid timetabling and subject specialization, ensures that children have only minimal contact with their form teachers. Children thus deprived have insufficient opportunities for establishing stable relationships over a period of time with the one person who is nominally responsible for their general progress.

Thus failure to teach children to read results in part from a buck-passing attitude on the part of school personnel. Secondary teachers shrug their shoulders and reflect on the incompetence of their junior colleagues who, in turn, accuse infant staff of letting children play all day and neglecting the essentials. What is needed is a much more positive contribution and an awareness of what sheer misery faces the nonreader in junior or secondary schools. Day after day, year after year, he is faced with a succession of tasks which are beyond him. Every day piles up new failures to a stock which is already large. What a round of dreary monotony must each school day bring – a few menial jobs maybe which are all he is considered capable of, but nothing really learned, until the will to learn ceases altogether and the only reactions to school are withdrawal or antisocial behaviour. The latter symptoms are the nonreader's verdict on teachers and schools, and if he could write he would scrawl in letters ten feet high, 'You teachers are wasting my time'. No wonder children burn down schools and vandalism grows apace. As a person, the nonreader becomes something less than human when all humans about him can read but he cannot. To his peers he is the class idiot, the butt of many jokes, an object of scorn and derision. What ideas and interests he has remain stunted. How can they grow (or how can he) without the aid of print? For him there is no chance of fun or escape such as we who read can enjoy. And what of his future? In the reading world of today, will he meet a partner who will gladly marry an illiterate? How will his children feel when they discover that their father cannot read? The chances are high that he will not marry at all or ever achieve satisfactory relationships with members of the opposite sex or make friends with members of his own. Failure to read today is not only a stigma, it is a passport to our ever enlarging dole queues and prisons. In a world in which opportunities for hewers of wood and drawers of water are diminishing rapidly due to mechanization and automation, what chance does the adult illiterate have of carving out for himself a satisfactory life? When graduates cannot get jobs these days, what hope is there for the nonreader?

Illiteracy will not be eradicated without compassion on the part of teachers, and a sensitivity which enables them to project themselves inside the personality of the nonreader. Only when they see what an abyss of waste and unfulfilment lies there will they realize what a life of shame and degradation is the illiterate's lot. Sensitivity and compassion are the roots of attitudes important in teaching the nonreader. However, tears of sorrow for the world's unfortunates are no help if the will and professional competence to put matters right are lacking. How competently have we tackled the problem of illiteracy in the past? It is odd, but it seems that we have generally tended to use approaches which are almost guaranteed to fail. Remedial teaching needs to be tackled in an organized way with sufficient time and resources to do the job regularly and well. In practice it is rarely tackled thus. If attempted by the class teacher in the junior school, it is usually fitted in at odd moments and is the first thing to go when other pressures build up. Worse, in many junior schools, teachers have abdicated from their responsibilities towards the poor or non-readers altogether and delegate such work to visiting remedial specialists who withdraw the children periodically for instruction. Often there is no contact between visiting remedial specialist and regular class teacher. Thus the remedial work is done in isolation from the ongoing class work, and the class teacher, who in the junior school is with her pupils for almost the whole of each school day, fails to capitalize on the many opportunities for teaching reading, both formally and incidentally, which come her way. In larger junior and secondary schools remedial departments withdraw the poorer readers for some time each day, or, if the school is streamed, into separate remedial classes. The latter tend to be extremely hetrogeneous in age and, as they usually turn out to be collections of the school's problem children, difficulties of a nonreading kind obtrude on the task of teaching reading. Additionally, such complete withdrawal from the normal interests, expectations and activities of peer groups in ordinary classes carries its own stigma and results in standards of achievement being unrealistically low. If a school with ten teachers has twenty nonreaders, the latter would surely have a better chances of success if every teacher had two each rather than one teacher having all twenty. All forms of withdrawal of children from ordinary classes for remedial instruction have one certain result—they remove from the persons (class and form teachers) who spend most time with the children concerned, any opportunities for acquiring interest in, experience of, and responsibility for teaching reading.

I have already remarked that the majority of our secondary schools, because of the ways in which they are organized and staffed, are not the best of places in which to start learning to read. It takes most of the infant school period to give a child sufficient opportunities to provide evidence of failing in reading. There is left only one obvious stage in the educational system where remedial reading can be done effectively – in the junior school. The majority of junior schools are organized by age groups into separate classes each with their own teacher for most of each school day. The class teacher is the one who knows the children best, is thus best fitted to teach them to read, and has the greatest number of opportunities to do it. The best time of all is in the first junior year before failure has become totally ingrained and the motivation of a fresh start in new conditions still offers hope and stimulus. If the first junior year became the 'reading year' with all else subordinated to it, there would be little need for the expensive superstructure of remedial provision at subsequent stages of schooling.

The status quo in reading, as I see it, is full of imperfections and matters will be slow to improve. A considerable period of time will be needed to effect the necessary changes in teacher training, teacher attitude and school organization. Meanwhile, many teachers at every stage of the educational system are deeply concerned that children in their charge are unable to read and that they themselves lack the training and expertise to help them. For these and many others in the painful process of trial and error alluded to earlier, it is hoped that the following expression of seven basic principles will be a useful guide when teaching the nonreader:

1 *Remove all associations with previous failure* i.e. teach him by approaches which are completely new to him.
2 After failing for so long *the child must begin to be rewarded by success*, and the work must so develop that reward (success) is fed in at each new learning step.
3 *The teaching must be individualized* Rarely will one child's reading needs and problems at any one time be precisely the same as those of another and therefore teaching poor or nonreaders in groups will seldom be effective.
4 *The teaching must be regular* Working by fits and starts or fitting it in at odd moments is of no use. A regular, systematic pattern of short, frequent sessions is needed and, once begun, must be maintained.
5 *The teacher must have confidence in the methods used* She must show that she means business and that she can deliver the goods. Children who have failed many times are hesitant at each new beginning and suspicious of, and uncooperative towards, those who teach half-heartedly.
6 *A dynamic approach is essential* Remedial approaches with older children are ineffective when they ape too closely the methods commonly used with infant school beginners. Thus hearing children read, page by page, through a reading scheme, which may be fine with five or six year olds, must seem a long and laborious business to children of nine or ten, or to secondary pupils. What is needed is quite spectacular success, especially in the early stages. This is necessary to give the child confidence in his own ability to succeed and to enable him to bring interest, effort and determination to bear when occasionally the going gets rough.
7 *Start with the child's own language* There are few suitable books on which the older beginner can usefully make a start. He has almost certainly been put off before by books. In any case, books contain the printed speech and ideas of others, whereas the only functional language with which the nonreader has any confidence at all is his own. It may be, and usually is, extremely limited, but it contains the only words he uses, needs and finds important, and therefore a reading scheme based on it offers the greatest chance for early success.

Though the majority of teachers would probably agree in theory with these principles, in practice they are deterred from applying them largely by lack of confidence in themselves. This is explained partly by the inadequate training which the majority of junior/secondary teachers have received; by the diminished status of reading vis-à-vis other school subjects; by ignorance of simple, direct techniques; and by the growth of a mystique which shrouds remedial teaching with a cloak of pseudoscientific jargon. The latter provides opportunities for teachers to take refuge behind excuses such as the child is linguistically deprived; emotionally disturbed; lacks confidence; cannot make effort; has poor retention; has missed the beginnings; has a poor home background; is word blind; or is not ready. All these reflect negative attitudes towards teaching reading and are in fact reasons for not teaching reading since they are frequently euphemisms for 'I don't know how to teach them'. It may be that a given child has many handicaps. If so, we do little that is positive by dwelling on these. Rather, the best starting point is to consider the child's strengths (few though they may be) and to work from there. There are, of course, children who suffer from a multiplicity of handicaps – physical, psychological and social – or from single handicaps of such severity that educational provision out of the ordinary school is required. For these the teaching of reading is an irrelevance until their various disorders are put right. There still remain many children in ordinary schools who appear normal in most respects except that they cannot read. There is nothing greatly wrong with their intelligence and powers of perception and coordination when they can see, hear and speak, get themselves to and from school safely, and take part successfully in various activities, such as ball games, which require considerable skill. It is for such nonreaders that I wish to recommend a simple teaching method based on the seven principles enumerated above. I have personally applied this method successfully to children categorized as severely subnormal, educationally subnormal, to nonreaders in ordinary schools and to illiterate adults. Some hundreds of teachers trained by me at initial and in-service courses can also testify to the efficacy of this method.

A speech-based individualized remedial approach
The following materials are required: two large sheets of card about 255 × 305 mm, a pencil, a ruler, two black felt tip pens, a pair of scissors, two foolscap envelopes and a scribbling pad. Rule off the cards with horizontal pencilled lines about 20 mm apart.

Stages of teaching
1 Get the child talking. Any topic which interests him will do. If necessary prod him with appropriate questions until he has given

about a dozen sentences or remarks. As he talks, write down fast on your scribbling pad exactly what he says.

2 Read back aloud from your pad what he has said as soon as he has finished talking.

3 Print boldly in pencil on one of the ruled cards his speech in exact word and sentence order. Transcribe this from the scribbling pad, taking care to keep each sentence to a separate space between the lines.

4 Say each word aloud as you print it, having your pupil repeat the word after you.

5 As the printing of each sentence is completed, read it aloud in full and get the child to repeat it after you.

6 Once the speech has been completely printed, read the whole thing through aloud, asking the child to join in with you.

7 Give the child a felt pen. Ask him to trace with it over your pencilled print, saying each word aloud as he 'writes' it. As each sentence is traced ask him to read it in full. When the whole thing has been traced, ask him to read it in full, helping him where necessary.

8 While the child is tracing and reading from his card, make an exact duplicate in felt pen on the other.

9 Cut your card into sentence strips, shuffle them and present them to him in random order.

10 The child matches the strips to the traced sentences on his own card, reading them aloud as he does so. Help him if necessary.

11 When the master card has been completely covered with the sentence strips, take back all the strips, shuffle them and place them between you to play the sentence game. Take one each of the foolscap envelopes. Print your name on one and your pupil's name on the other. Turn over the master card to remove contextual and sentence order clues. Flash the sentence strips. Each one read perfectly goes into the pupil's envelope. Those where difficulty is apparent go into yours.

12 When all the sentence strips have been thus treated, remove from your envelope the strips which require further work and reinforce these by further repetition, matching to the master card and reading aloud.

13 Repeat the sentence game until all sentence strips are successfully transferred to the pupil's envelope.

14 Cut up the sentence strips into their separate words, asking the child to read each word as you cut it off.

15 Shuffle the words and present them in random order, getting the child to match each word to the master card, and reading it aloud as he finds it in context.

16 When the master card has been completely covered with the matched individual words, start to play the word game. Turn

over the master card to remove contextual aid. Place all the words between you, shuffle them, and present them in random order. All words read accurately at sight go into the pupil's envelope while all those read incorrectly go into yours.

17 When all the words have been transferred to the respective envelopes, take those from your envelope and reinforce the learning of these by further repetition, matching to the master card and reading aloud.

18 Repeat the word game reinforcement procedure until every word is read perfectly at sight.

Development of wider reading
Repeat the above procedures by processing further spoken sentences on a variety of topics until a sight vocabulary of three to four hundred words has been achieved. Do not rush your pupil into printed books and do not insult his maturity by offering him infantile material. Start with the *Radio Times* or *TV Times*. He will be much more motivated to find out 'what's on the telly' each night than to follow the 'adventures' of the various cats, dogs and small children depicted in the typical infant reading schemes. The first printed book offered should reflect what, by then, you will know of his particular interests. As will be seen in the case study below, the first real book read by one of my adult illiterates was the *Highway Code*. It is extremely difficult material but he mastered it. He had to – to take his driving test.

At about the time when imported language from printed texts is introduced and a start made on weaning the pupil away from his own speech as the basis of reading development, a start should be made with phonic work. Only when this has been done systematically will your pupil have the independence to tackle new words with confidence. Teach him always, of course, to use context first. He will have already proved to himself the efficacy of this and had ample practice at it by matching words and sentences to his master card. Context is the most important clue to meaning and therefore to recognition, but when this fails he must apply his word attack skills. With my own pupils I refer to word attack as 'spelling', for I always insist on them writing each new word when they have built it. Writing is reading's sister skill and the one reinforces the other. Each new word made and written goes into the word stock for later practice and consolidation. Start the phonic work by drawing on the spoken vocabulary already read. Establish rules within this area before applying them to new words, taking care to teach the correct sounds, phonic not alphabetic, with consonants unvoiced. Teachers unsure of themselves at this stage and concerned not to omit important steps in phonic progression could keep to the stages advocated by A. E. Tansley (1967) in *Reading and Remedial Reading*. Teachers can be reassured that pupils trained on the methods suggested will rarely have to start from scratch in phonic work. The kinesthetic element (tracing), the writing and fequent repetition built in will result in the majority of pupils having acquired an implicit knowledge of many of the major sounds and symbols and the ability to apply this knowledge successfully to new words. Care should be taken not to overburden the pupils with phonics. It is better done regularly in short doses, say one new rule a day with occasional revision of previous work or a game thrown in where suitable from Stott's (1962) *Programmed Reading Kit*.

Advantages of speech-based reading approach

1   There is a systematic structure of teaching stages
The successive procedures described can be grouped into three phases:

1   speaking and tracing
2   sentence matching and reading
3   word matching and reading.

This pattern helps the teacher to allocate time regularly with clear targets to aim at each day. Thus a week's work could be planned and executed on the following basis:

Monday	Speaking and tracing (preparing thc materials).
Tuesday	Sentence matching and reading.
Wednesday	Word matching and reading. This is a much more
Thursday	complex process than operations at the sentence stage and therefore more time is needed.
Friday	Reinforcement and application of words and sentences learned by illustrating, modelling, captioning etc.

2   The teaching is personalized
This is much more than individualized teaching. The latter often means little more than teaching a child on his own but doing it with materials to which the child has to be fitted and which have not necessarily been designed with the particular child in mind. Where the teaching is personalized the materials arise from the child's own resources and in the speech-based approach are actually made by the child himself. Thus the level of pupil involvement is extremely high. Not only does he provide the content, he actually makes his own reading scheme (the master cards). Additionally a fool-proof recording system (the word and sentence envelopes) is built in to the teaching procedure. At any time both teacher and pupil can evaluate their joint progress, see what they have achieved and what yet remains to be done.

Because the teaching is personalized the chances of failure, as compared with traditional approaches, are reduced. There are no difficulties about levels of content and interest. There are no books, and no unfamiliar language structures or situations are introduced. This is a distinct advantage over the traditional reading primer where many of the situations are contrived and artificial and much of the language stilted and unnatural due to the necessity to build in a high rate of repetition. Reinforcement is much more wide-ranging than in typical look and say methods and includes a kinesthetic element (tracing), a functional discrimination element (matching), and play (sentence and word games).

3   The method is simple

It requires no previous experience or training in the teaching of reading. It can be applied successfully at any stage in junior, middle or secondary school by the nonspecialist teacher to get the nonreader off to a good start.

A case study

The exposition given above of the stages of the speech-based reading approach is necessarily analytical and gives a somewhat clinical air to a method which in practice is warm and lively and gives a high degree of job satisfaction. The feeling that she is succeeding when all others have failed before is a great source of professional pride and stimulus to the teacher. Also, as the content of the reading scheme develops from the pupil's own resources of speech, ideas and interests, the teacher has opportunities, which few other methods offer, to observe her pupil closely and to get to know him not only as reader and learner but also as a person. At later stages, as when the pupil is weaned away from his own limited speech and range of experience into the wider world of printed books, this pupil knowledge can be put to good effect in the selection of appropriate reading matter and also in the development of new and wider interests from those which exist already. These points are exemplified in the treatment of Malcolm, an eighteen year old illiterate.

Malcolm's case has been chosen because he had been remote from school influences for over three years, after some ten years of reading failure in school, so he would normally be expected to pose greater problems for the reading teacher than a younger child of school age. His record of failure is longer and his negative attitude towards books and reading more ingrained. His mother died a week after he was born and his father, already responsible for two older children of school age, could not cope satisfactorily with such a young baby. At age four months Malcolm was adopted by his late mother's best friend, a lady whose own three children were already in their teens. Students of child development will be aware of the links between lack of mothering in the first few months of life and later linguistic impairment and personality damage. Malcolm, in fact, at age four months was already a potential nonreader. However, since then he has been brought up as the baby in a stable family. He was a sickly child and had frequent, though not prolonged, absences from infant school. He was also a quiet child, somewhat withdrawn, with few friends. This was unfortunate for Malcolm's own personal development. Had he been aggressive, given to tantrums and defiance he would have called to himself the teacher attention which he obviously needed. But he was 'good', i.e. did not talk in class, or anywhere else for that matter. And he 'behaved', i.e. did not cause disciplinary problems in school. He was also 'reliable', i.e. could be entrusted with numerous menial tasks. These occupied most of his school time which could have been better devoted to learning. Numerous parental visits to infant school to seek help or advice on what to do about Malcolm's lack of progress in reading elicited the invariable response—'he is not ready yet'. The readiness excuse was usually accompanied by politely expressed implications of parental overanxiety. In junior school the implications were made more directly. Self-help within the family was resorted to. Malcolm was read to in bed every evening and was periodically forced, page by page, through infant primers, but to no avail. By the time when Malcolm was transferred to secondary school the family were resigned to the fact that Malcolm was just 'slow' and would probably never read. It seems incredible that in none of the three schools which he attended was any attempt made at referral for special educational provision or remedial treatment. For ten long years, through infant, junior and secondary school, Malcolm sat quietly and was 'good', and did odd jobs, and nobody ever taught him to read or write. In the three years since leaving school he has had seventeen different jobs. In each case he has been sacked for incompetence, or apathy or lack of concentration. He has no confidence in himself as a person and appears incapable of making strong effort to succeed at anything worthwhile. I am astonished that he has not developed delinquent tendencies. Fortunately, he has a strong interest in mechanical contraptions, especially cars and motorbikes, and with these he has undoubted ability. He can strip down a car engine and rebuild it as easily as the average youth can repair a puncture in the tyre of his pushbike. This interest and mechanical ability have been his salvation. He has his own motorbike which he maintains and repairs. It is his only status symbol and it brings him prestige with his very small circle of peers. When faults develop in their machines, they rely on Malcolm to diagnose the trouble and put them right.

When I was asked to see if I could teach him to read, I enquired about previous efforts by others to do this. I was given his life history as recorded above, and told how both foster parents and the eldest foster brother had made repeated but unsuccessful attempts to interest him but that he could not be motivated. I suggested that over a period of time they should drop frequent hints to him that if he could read he could get a job in a garage and then, by night school or day release, acquire the qualifications necessary to become a skilled mechanic. Malcolm had previously shunned any prospect of skilled work because his inability to read precluded any possibility of acquiring paper qualifications. I also learned that, though a good driver and fanatically keen on motorcycling, he was still driving on L plates. He had already had four provisional licences and had not many more to run and yet he could not apply for a driving test because of his inability to study and learn the Highway Code. I suggested, therefore, that the family should cautiously drop hints about him taking his driving test and about the necessity for him to learn to read in order to do this.

After a time he rose to the bait and I was introduced to him as a reading expert. I explained to him that it was as easy for me to teach people to read as it was for him to strip down a motorbike engine. I told him that he would learn to read quite a lot within the next half hour – and he did. First I explained that in order to teach him I needed to know one or two things about him. I asked him to tell me about himself: his name, address, and what he liked doing best. As he told me, I scribbled it down fast. When he had finished speaking I read his words back to him. He agreed that this is what he had said:

My name is Malcolm Bloggs. (The name and address are fictitious)
I live at 14 Roman Crescent, Redtown.
I am eighteen years old.
I am keen on motorbikes.
My bike needs a rebore.
It is a Suzuki 100.
I got it last year.
It was brand new when I got it.
It cost £200.
Some carbon dropped off the piston.
The carbon scored the barrel.
I took it to pieces.
I need a barrel and piston.
Then I can rebuild it.
I have sent for these parts to the reborers.
They will cost about £5.

On one of my ready-ruled cards I wrote these sentences in pencil in bold print, keeping each sentence on a separate line. As I printed each word I said it aloud, asking Malcolm to repeat it after me. Each completed sentence was read aloud by me and repeated after me by Malcolm. When his speech was completely transferred from my pad to the ruled card, I gave him a black felt pen and asked him to trace with it over the pencilled print. I made him read each word and sentence as he traced it. While he was tracing and reading I made an exact duplicate of the master card in black felt pen. When he had finished 'writing' I asked him to read with me what he had written. He made a good attempt with few hesitations. We discussed each error and I asked him to read a second time. This he did with almost complete success.

I then took the card which I had written (not his traced one) and cut with large scissors along the line into sentence strips, reading each sentence as I cut it. I shuffled the strips and flashed them to him in random order. Those which he read at sight were matched to his own traced card and placed on top in the appropriate places. Those with which he had difficulty were kept back and flashed again until he read them and matched them perfectly on the master card.

Then we played the sentence game. I had two large envelopes, one for Malcolm and one for me. The sentence strips were removed from the master card, placed between us and shuffled. I flashed them to him in random order. Each one he read correctly was put in his envelope. I put in my envelope those sentence strips which were read incorrectly. When all the sentence strips had been dealt, we had in the two envelopes a record on the one hand of all sentences read correctly, and on the other hand a record of those which required further work. These were then discussed, read, and matched to the master card. We then used these strips for the second round of the sentence game. This time all the sentence strips were successfully transferred to his envelope. We were both now entirely confident that he could read the sentences even in random order.

Next we played the word game. All the sentence strips were cut up into individual words. They were used as flash cards until all were read correctly (with some words several repetitions were needed) and matched to the master card. The two envelopes were used again, this time for the individual words. These were shuffled and placed in a pile between us. As they were flashed to him, he put in his envelope those which he read correctly, while I put in mine those which he failed to read accurately. Further flash card and matching work was done with these until, at the end of the second round, his envelope was full and mine was empty. He knew and could read all the words. We counted them and found that there were eighty-eight words arranged in sixteen sentences. Many of the words were repeated several times. His actual sight vocabulary acquired in this first teaching session was sixty-two separate words. These are reproduced alphabetically in the table below, the numbers in brackets referring to the frequency of use of the word which they follow:

A   a(3), about, am(2), and, at.
B   barrel(2), bike, bikes, Bloggs, brand.
C   can, carbon(2), cost(2), Crescent.
D   dropped.
E   —
F   five, for
G   got(2).
H   have.
I   I(9), is(2), it(7).
J   —
K   keen.
L   last, live.
M   Malcolm, motor, My (2).
N   name, need, needs, new.
O   off, old, on.
P   parts, pieces, piston(2), pounds(2).
Q   —
R   rebore, reborers, rebuild, Redtown.
S   sent, scored, some, Suzuki.
T   The, the(3), Then, these, to(2), took.
U   —
V   —
W   was, when, will.
X   —
Y   years, years.
Z   —
Numbers read: 14, 18, 100, 200

When Malcolm and I together counted the words and sentences he had read in this first teaching session he was obviously delighted with his own prowess, and he promised me before I left that he would sit with his eldest brother and practice all the world flash cards for five or ten minutes every day for a week until I could come again.

On my second session with him it was obvious that he had done his homework. He read his master card perfectly and with great confidence and knew every word flash card at sight. I now needed more of Malcolm's oral speech. I encouraged him to talk about motorbikes, and as he told me, I wrote it down. This is what he said:

My hobby is repairing motorbikes.
I did one for a lad last week.
He broke down in Fordtown.
The cam chain snapped.
I had to strip it all down.
Some pieces were in the gear box.

Some were in the sump.
I had to get another cam chain and rebuild it.
I also do sand racing.
I won three cups last year.
I have to go to Blackpool for them.
I get them on Christmas Eve.
I go sand racing at Fleetwood and Redcar.
I also go to Hartlepool and Southport.
Southport is very good.

This material was treated in exactly the same way as his oral communication of the week before. I wrote in print. He traced. The master card was read and my card cut into sentence strips. The envelopes were brought out and used for the sentence game and then for the word game. He worked very hard and was as confident in his own ability to learn as he was in my ability to teach him.

Between this and the third session homework was done faithfully and regularly, and reinforcement of all words learned in the first two sessions was proved by his 100 per cent success rate when I tested all the words at the start of my third visit. In this session the following material was elicited from Malcolm:

I got my bike back on Saturday.
I had it on the road on Sunday.
I went to Roy Dell at Pudsey, near Leeds.
I had to go on the train.
The fare was £1.55 pence return.
The parts were there.
They cost £16.
It goes all right now.
I had to borrow £9.
My mum lent it me.
I'm going to pay her back about a pound a week.

These sentences were treated in the by now familiar stages of writing and tracing, matching, and sentence and word games. Towards the end of this session I had no doubt of Malcolm's motivation or of his confidence in me and in himself. He was concentrating and could already make sustained effort. I promised him that the next time I came I would make some special books for him to read. I made the books as we went along in the fourth session. I had previously prepared some cards for motor car identification. These were pictures cut from one of the Ladybird Books of motor cars. (I did not dare to use the actual books in case he associated these with school situations and with small children learning to read. Nothing deters the older nonreader more than reading matter which is apparently in-

111

fantile.) I cut out twenty well-known cars and mounted the pictures on separate cards. He recognized the majority of them by their identifying characteristics and we worked on the others until he knew them well. I then printed on separate cards the names of all the cars, reading them aloud as I wrote. He then matched each card to the appropriate picture, with some help from me. Both sets of cards (pictures and flash cards) were shuffled and presented to him in random order. After two or three rounds he could read the names of all the cars without the pictures. These were the first words which he read for me which did not actually issue originally from his own lips. They were introduced in order to widen his sight vocabulary. We also used the pictures and captions to play word and picture snap.

I then took the pictures of the following: a Ford Anglia, a Reliant Regal, a Fiat 500, a Hillman Imp, a Mini and an Austin 1100 and stuck them, along with their accompanying captions, each on a separate card. I printed a few sentences about each, reading them aloud as I wrote. For example, the card with the Ford Anglia picture and caption had the following accompanying sentences:

This is a yellow one with a white top.
It has a 998 c.c. engine.
It seats four people.
It has a top speed of about 70 miles per hour.
This one is the de luxe model.

This card, together with the others which were stapled into a Book of Cars, made possible the learning of expressions such as: two-cylinder, 499 c.c. engine; very economical; runs on two-star petrol; rear-engined; independent suspension; overall length; fibreglass body; maximum speed; front-mounted engine; four passengers; hydrolastic fluid suspension; sideways-mounted engine; front wheel drive. Malcolm made a creditable attempt at most of these, which I prescribed for homework along with all word flash cards previously learned.

Apart from cars and motorbikes, Malcolm's only other interest in life was watching television. By the start of my fifth session with him I judged that it was time that this interest was harnessed to the cause of his reading development. Accordingly I asked him to bring me the evening paper and I turned to the broadcasting section. I found that the names of most of the popular tv programmes were within his spoken vocabulary. I read to him the times and names of the programmes scheduled for that evening. He joined in and repeated them with me and he was soon able to read them independently.

During this session we made a new reading card. I cut out from a motorcycle journal a picture of the front wheel assembly of a machine exactly similar to the model owned by Malcolm, and mounted the picture on a large card, leaving a wide margin all round. I asked him to name the different parts and as he named them I captioned them in the margin, drawing lines to link the names to the actual parts. The names were reproduced as separate flash cards which were then matched to the words on the card. After a short time he was able to read the flash cards in random order with 100 per cent success with the master card withdrawn.

I now judged that it was time to begin to wean Malcolm away from home-made reading matter to commercially printed material. The only examples he had previously met were the TV programmes in the newspaper. I thought it was time that he had his first proper book. I brought out the Highway Code and we started to learn the road signs. He knew many of these empirically but had previously not been able to read any of the words associated with them. From these we went on to lane markings and braking distances. These sections of the Highway Code, plus all words previously learned, were his homework assignment for the coming week. He also had to read each evening the TV programmes in the broadcasting section of the newspaper.

We started the sixth session by revising the sections of the Highway Code practised the previous week and went on to tackle a new chapter – 'The road user on wheels'. I had decided that this week I would begin to build in the phonic skills. We spread out on the table every word flash card he had ever had, and I asked him to pick out words in which the short (open) vowel associated with the symbols A, a occurred. We did this systematically with the other short vowel sounds.

Over the next few weeks we extended our reading of the Highway Code and built up our phonic progressions. For example, in the seventh session I taught him the correct (unvoiced) sounds of the single consonants into simple three-letter words. I asked him to lip-read me as I said each word softly and then to whisper each word to himself as he wrote it. He had surprisingly little difficulty. In subsequent weeks we systematically tackled the long vowel and vowel digraph sounds, blending them with the single consonant sounds he already knew. The early phonic word was tackled in the following sequence:

1 *Simple short (open) vowels* – a, e, i, o, u, both capital and lower case forms.
2 *Single consonants* – b, c (k sound), d, f, g (hard), h, j, k, l, m, n, p, r, s, t, v, w, y, z.
3 *Closed (long) vowels* – 'magic e' modifying the vowels a, i, o, u. The influence of the e in softening c and g, as in 'face' and 'page', was taught simultaneously.
4 ai, ay, ee, ea; oa.

5   oo (both sounds); ow and ou as in 'cow' and 'out'; oi and oy as in 'oil' and 'boy'.
6   ar; er, ir, ur; or.

On this basis of the common vowel sounds were then built the double consonant blends and consonant digraphs. They were taught in the following sequence as initial blends: bl, br, cl, cr, dr, fl, fr, gl, gr, pl, pr, sc, sk, sl, sm, sn, sp, st, sw, tr, tw, ch, sh, th (both sounds). Qu and x were then taught.

Examples of the blends and digraphs were drawn from his word flash card sight vocabulary initially, and as he gained expertise the rules were applied to words not previously read. Each new word was lipread as I mouthed it. I asked him to map each word mentally and then to write it, whispering the word as he wrote. Though there were occasional lapses he was generally confident and the vast majority of his responses were correct. When errors did occur they arose from overconfidence and I judged this no bad thing.

He absolutely raced through the next stage of building words with double consonant endings, using the following sequence: ck, ff, ft, lt, ll, mp, nd, ng, nk, nt, sh, st, ss, sk, sp, th, ch.

At the moment of writing this I have had ten hours of teaching contact time with Malcolm. He can read with understanding almost everything in the Highway Code and is so confident with it that he has applied for his driving test. He has extended his newspaper reading from the broadcasting section to the motorcycles for sale, wanted, and accessories advertising columns, and he also regularly reads the jobs column under 'garage work' in the hope of getting work as a trainee mechanic. I hope to be able to help Malcolm a lot further along the reading road. He will never be the world's greatest reader. I doubt if I will ever get him to read for pleasure. At least he is no longer frightened of books, he wants to read and I am confident that he will be able to read sufficiently well to satisfy his own purposes and to cope with the reading necessary to the functional situations in which he finds himself.

In discussing the case of Malcolm and others like him with groups of teachers and reading experts, colleagues are invariably swift to point out the importance of motivation as the greatest impetus in beginning reading. I always hasten to agree, but point out that the possibility of motivation had always been there. Malcolm had been interested in things mechanical since infancy but no one in the whole of his school career had harnessed that interest to the cause of his reading development. By sticking to my seven basic remedial reading principles I had been able to do in ten hours what had been proved impossible to achieve in ten years in school.

There are some slight differences between the treatment of Malcolm and what is possible in the school situation. For a number of reasons I was only able to teach Malcolm once a week and I had to depend on others, especially his eldest foster brother, to carry out the regular reinforcement (homework) which was necessary. In school it is possible for the teacher to organize this herself by phasing the work over a whole week with a specified area each day, as suggested earlier in this chapter. There are also available in school greater opportunities for reinforcement by various forms of creative expression.

In conclusion, I feel that, though this approach has much to offer to those who might not otherwise read at all, it has also much to give to the teacher herself. As teachers, our roles are so diffuse that our failures are more frequent than our successes. If in the field of remedial reading we can succeed where once we failed, can experience the satisfaction of a job well done and done with some pleasure, our possible failures in noncognitive fields might be judged less harshly, both by ourselves and by society at large.

Part 4

Organizing for reading extension

Many agencies contribute to setting up the conditions in which reading extension can develop most favourably. Each stage of schooling has its part to play, as do the LEAS, the publishers and the researchers. The contribution of each of these agencies is discussed in Chapter 9. The bodies who can play the most effective part in developing expertise and appropriate professional attitudes in the teaching force are the various training establishments. Chapter 9 also examines the role of the colleges and university departments of education and suggests ways in which current practice may be improved.

Chapter 9

Organizing for reading extension

The infant school

Though this book is directed at schools beyond the infant stage, I am aware that many of the ideas in it could be adopted by teachers in infant schools. I am also aware that, if those ideas germinate and become widely accepted in practice in junior and secondary schools, it would be helpful for infant teachers to be familiar with likely development at those stages and thus to be able to prepare their pupils more relevantly for junior school. It is a premise of this book that the development of the higher order reading skills depends on the prior establishment of basic competence, the sort of competence which the typical infant school aims to achieve. Now there is great danger in assigning to different stages of education teaching roles which are too sharply differentiated from those at adjacent stages. This is evident in the historical attitude to beginning reading which characterizes many junior schools, an attitude which in practice assigns the task of teaching beginning reading to the infant school only and therefore identifies that task as one from which teachers at later stages of schooling may opt out. However, if infant schools are content to accept only a minimal role in reading development, such compartmentalization would result in many children not having acquired good early attitudes towards reading.

Admittedly to get the majority of infant school pupils to the stage of competence required to complete the typical infant reading scheme is in itself no mean feat. However, for many infant schools this is the final goal and any attempt to do more is rare. The dilemma which many infant teachers face at this stage is a real one. They have got certain children to a level of performance on which junior schools should be able to build adequately. They have also other children coming up who are much below this standard and who will require considerable work to achieve it. Realistically the infant teachers regard their classes as a series of layers. Once the children in the top layer have been worked up to a certain point they are given the freedom of the library, encouraged to read widely and directed to writing activities, usually of an individual kind. Work can then proceed with the next layer to bring them up to the same standard.

Though it is difficult to generalize when no two schools are alike, from my own experience as an infant teacher, as a primary head and as one who, over the last five years, has visited in one capacity or another over a hundred different infant schools, there is discernible a pattern by which the majority of teachers structure the infant reading course. It falls into the following four stages:

1 *Prereading:* a series of activities and experiences which enable the teacher to ensure that the formal teaching of reading can be started with success and confidence.
2 *Look and say teaching:* usually with a commercially produced reading scheme, progress through which establishes and extends the sight vocabulary, largely by repetition.
3 *Phonic teaching:* the common blends and letter strings developed through the reading scheme, and supplemented by games and apparatus.
4 *Independence:* when the child has completed the official reading scheme and is encouraged to exploit the library and read books of many different kinds.

Though the work is frequently done with groups, in my experience, the commonest method once formal reading begins is to hear each individual child read as frequently as possible. This is certainly necessary at certain stages to test the child's ability and to assess readiness for further learning steps. However, in my opinion, such individualization is not necessary throughout every page of every book in the reading scheme. If protracted, the practice of verbalization is reinforced and the capacity to read silently and at speed is thereby reduced. The emphasis is on correct recognition and pronunciation and there is no general awareness on the part of infant teachers of the need for the intelligent anticipation which characterizes the very good reader. All that is being suggested here is that, given suitable training, infant teachers could begin to incorporate oral discussion methods such as prediction and deletion exercises with selected groups. Probably this would be well received by the brighter readers or those who have graduated through the reading scheme to the freedom of the library. These children are often neglected in favour of the up-and-coming layer and would benefit from occasional stretching exercises by which silent reading would be promoted and the beginnings of the questioning attitude essential to critical reading could be encouraged.

The junior/middle school
The junior school is the stage when all the conditions for reading extension are most favourable. The majority of the children can at least read silently and at a literal level of comprehension with simple

material. They are with their teacher for most of each school day. Given adequate training, and sufficient reading time with children, teachers should be able to exploit a wide range of teaching situations in which group work and individual work and oral and written activity are nicely balanced, and attention can be given to critical reading, to reading efficiency through individual skill development, and to the growth of the habit of reading, both for information and pleasure. If reading is to have the attention it deserves, it needs to be elevated to the status it once had in our schools and to be regarded as a super-subject. It therefore needs the most favourable learning time, ideally the period before midmorning break, and this should be regularly timetabled. Where reading is done at all in junior schools at the present time it is a haphazard, often incidental affair and liable to be omitted altogether for the most trifling reasons. To guard against this the reading lesson, a daily hour, should be regarded as inviolate, and not to be missed except for the most compelling reasons. Teachers, especially those in today's primary schools, have become so used to freedom in the classroom that the word 'timetable' has become a term of odium and is equated with all that was formal and repressive in the traditional schools of long ago. However, schools exist not to extend the freedom of the teacher, but so that children may learn. They need time to learn. In order to guarantee that important things are learned well, time has to be allocated in proportion to the relative importance of subjects. Some subjects are more important than others. Society expects that children in our schools become literate and numerate, whatever else they may do. As literacy is basic to the learning of almost every subject in school, reading should have priority over all other subjects. The only positive way to guarantee such priority is by reflecting its importance in the timetable. One hour each school day is no more than a suitable index of the importance of reading vis-à-vis the other subjects in school.

Timetabling and subject divisions came rightly into disrepute in the 1930s when conditions were vastly different from those in junior schools today. In 1937 it was quite proper for the *Handbook of Suggestions* to point out that 'a subject deals largely, as it must, with generalized experience which may have no appeal to the young child, and for him any division of experience into separate timetable subjects is at best an artificial business and in any case results in a great deal of his school work becoming unreal and lacking in any purpose he can comprehend'. Nowadays it is the complete lack of structure in most school work that has resulted in the work itself becoming unreal and lacking in any purpose that the children can comprehend. The NUT (1958) gave a salutary warning that 'arithmetic, though it can and must be given reality, has its own logical development, and any incidental treatment in terms of an accidental demand in pursuing a topic may lead to confusion and profitless meandering'.

The warning was heeded and though arithmetic has now become mathematics, the logical structure is still there and the necessity to timetable it as a separate subject, and usually at the most favourable time each day, is accepted in the majority of junior schools. It is unfortunate that no one has spoken up in such terms for the cause of reading, for surely a great deal of what is done in schools today in the name of reading can only be described as 'confusion and profitless meandering'.

The 1959 Primary Report (Ministry of Education 1959) which contained much more commonsense than many other government reports on education, has much to say about the effective use of time. It saw the timetable as 'a convenient framework within which the school can function'; as 'an expression of his (the head's) educational philosophy and that of his colleagues; it reduces to firm terms what they consider best for children and demonstrates their beliefs about the relative values of what the school has to offer.' It pointed out that 'in the allocation of time it is the head's duty to review the effects of his arrangements on the well-being of the children and staff and, as far as physical conditions allow, to make the timetable serve the educational ends he and his colleagues have set for themselves'. If reading is an important educational end it will figure prominently in the timetable. The Report saw the timetable as 'a framework, which holds the whole programme together, but which is never a straitjacket stifling initiative'. It pointed out that 'each aspect of education must have its proper share of time and attention' and that 'each day in school strenuous activity alternates with quieter pursuits and individual concentration with corporate endeavour. There must be time for the practice essential to learning and time for going back to revise and consolidate'. The Report also reminded us that 'the way in which time is used and work organized is a crucial factor in the development of a sense of purpose and of the self-discipline needed to pursue it'.

The 1959 Report also has a great deal to say about the concept of quality in education. It quotes the 'increasing attention' given by teachers to 'the worth of what is taught and to the quality of children's learning'. It states that 'the capacities of all children, dull and bright, must be exercised to the full', and that 'to achieve this end the work must be made interesting and a sense of standard must pervade it all'. We are reminded that 'no matter how excellent the equipment and materials, they will fail of their purpose unless the children learn effectively and learn what is of value. Whether or not they do this depends largely on the teacher's power to think ahead and organize.' The Report makes clear that 'the real objective (of education) is to give a good start in life to all the boys and girls in our primary and secondary schools. And from this point of view, it is the quality of the teachers, and of the teaching they give, that matters more in the long run than logistics.'

The Primary Report of 1959 has been drawn on heavily because of its constant insistence on the effective use of time and of the need for quality in both learning and teaching. Time and quality are what reading has lacked in the majority of our junior schools for over a generation. When time is insufficient low standards are almost inevitable. Even where standards are not exactly low it is doubtful if many children are being stretched to the highest levels of which they are capable. Though time is needed to teach anything well, what matters most is what is actually done in the time available. In the recent past, junior teachers have generally not known what it is possible for their pupils to achieve in reading. They have not known what to do even if the time has been there. It is hoped that the previous chapters will give teachers realistic aims to which they might aspire and a number of practical techniques by which their objectives may be realized. In asking for a timetabled reading lesson lasting an hour each day I am not advocating a return to the days when each subject had its own watertight compartment. I am only asking for the creation of conditions in which reading, the most basic of all school subjects, can be guaranteed the time and attention which are needed to teach it well. There is, after all, the rest of each school day to apply reading to the development of an everwidening range of interests, activities and experiences. This, of course, is one of the aims of teaching reading in the first place, and nothing better assists the capacity to integrate knowledge than the ability to read. Nor am I advocating any rigidity of practice in the organization of daily reading activities, for as the 1959 Report rightly points out 'with a rigid day to day plan many opportunities are missed'. Knowing what has to be done and given a battery of relevant techniques on which to draw, what is needed is the possibility of flexible arrangements of time and organization to achieve one's goals. For example, given an hour's reading time each day, teachers could readily ring the changes to suit their different purposes on a weekly timetable such as the one below for a hypothetical junior class of thirty-five children organized thus:

Group A 10 good readers
Group B 10 average to good readers
Group C 10 poor to average readers
Group D 5 poor readers

Group	Monday	Tuesday	Wednesday	Thursday	Friday	
					S	
A	*	X	X	X	H	
B	X	*	X	X	A	T
C	X	X	*	X	R	I
D	X	X	X	*	I	M
					N	E
					G	

Periods marked X are those when children work on their own at their reading laboratory cards, finding information for projects or at silent reading from library books.

The periods marked * are times when the teacher spends say thirty minutes exclusively in oral discussion activities with a single group. At this time the work could include prediction, deletion and SQ3R activities. The teacher has thus another thirty minutes of each reading period for individual work such as the evaluation of progress in laboratory exercises and promotion of individuals to new colour levels, speech-based approaches with slow readers and holding personal reading interviews. The Friday period is sharing time when various groups or individuals may contribute book reports, readings, dramatizations and the like.

It is difficult at this time to suggest appropriate organizational procedures for middle schools. The latter are at an early stage of evolution and can encompass an age range extending from eight to fourteen. This results in some middle schools being in effect junior schools in the traditional sense. Others, where the age range is ten to fourteen, are more closely aligned with ideas relating to the secondary field. Thus when discussing the middle school it is difficult to know whether specialization is to be deferred, as is likely in the majority of schools catering for the eight to twelve age group, or whether it is to be brought forward, a contingency which appears likely where middle schools cater for children up to fourteen years of age. In the case of those schools concerned with the middle years up to age twelve, there seems no reason why the suggestions relating to junior school practice should not prove helpful. Where middle school children can be as old as fourteen, the suggestions below for reading in secondary schools would probably be more appropriate.

The secondary school
There are four major deterrents to teaching reading in secondary schools.

First, most secondary teachers regard the teaching of reading as the responsibility of the primary school and generally consider reading as a specialism outside their area of competence. Such a view reflects traditional attitudes towards reading and inadequate preparation of personnel to teach it. In the past the major emphasis has been on the ability to decode. The 'reading for what' has not been stressed. As a result a situation appears to have arisen in which a proportion of children can read, but only with great difficulty. A higher proportion can read, but rarely choose to do so. To all intents and purposes the formal teaching of reading stops for most children at the end of the infant/beginning of the junior school stage.

Second, most secondary teachers are unfamiliar with the reading needs of their pupils. They fail to differentiate between those who, because of their slower learning rate, need a long-term programme adjusted to their particular needs and those for whom short-term treatment of a corrective kind is most appropriate.

Third, probably the greatest deterrent to teaching reading in the secondary school is the sheer absence of personnel trained to do it. This stems from the limited view of reading considered in point one above and the inadequacy and, in most cases, total absence of relevant training elements in college and university courses of the past.

Fourth, an area of major difficulty is the organization of secondary schools into separate subject departments. This sets up extreme difficulties in organizing a unified reading programme as compared with the primary school. In the latter the child is with his teacher for almost the whole of each school day and, knowing his reading strengths and weaknesses, the teacher can observe him, work with him, and help him in many different teaching and learning situations. In the secondary school generally no one knows the child well enough, or is in his company long enough, to be able to assume responsibility for his particular reading needs. Thus, whether a child needs a long-term programme of adjustment, short-term corrective treatment, or opportunities for enrichment are nobody's concern or responsibility.

The first three difficulties outlined above, need a thorough compulsory course for all intending secondary teachers as the only sure means of effecting improvements in reading. As for the fourth point, organization of secondary schools into separate subject areas need not pose the problems for teaching reading that it did formerly. The trend towards unstreaming, especially in comprehensive schools, is gathering momentum and should result in teachers having more time with the same groups of children each day. The organization proposed by Hutchinson and Young (1962) for the first two years of grammar school is also attracting adherents and will be the probable basis in many of the newly emerging middle schools.

However, changes in patterns of school organization are part of an evolutionary process and are necessarily slow. Rapid progress in improving reading teaching is most likely to be achieved by considering the peculiar needs of the secondary school and the part that reading can play by going along with the school and helping to satisfy those needs. Secondary school programmes are characterized by clearly defined subject disciplines. Each discipline has its own body of concepts and distinctive vocabulary which require development. Study activity becomes increasingly important and demands the acquisition of new sets of abilities. Libraries and resource centres are used as sources of information. The specialist content of the subject areas becomes increasingly difficult as regards concept level, vocabulary, sentence length and complexity and demands of the learner increased facility and precision in word perception and comprehension. Because the secondary pupil is subjected to many different types of reading, his own reading needs are diversified and he has to learn to adapt his reading to many different demands. Thus ability to adjust his speed and attack according to many different purposes is essential. He has to develop skill and independence in all aspects of study; setting himself realistic goals; locating information; and evaluating, selecting and organizing ideas according to his different purposes. The curricular demands of the secondary school make it important that teachers have the clearest and most relevant aims in teaching reading. They will necessarily be quite different from those appropriate at early stages of schooling and will result too in the need for a quite different set of teaching methods and materials.

The secondary school is already well placed from the point of view of implementing a daily reading lesson. All that is required is that one of the spaces in each day's form timetable be labelled 'reading'. The only other requirement is that personnel be trained to teach it. No one should be permitted to teach in a secondary school without a qualification in teaching reading. This is necessary to ensure that general reading development for all pupils continues from the primary stage to adulthood. The persons responsible for this should be the form teachers. In addition to contributing to all-round reading development, the secondary teacher who has had a course in the teaching of reading has great scope for improving the teaching of his own subject, whatever his specialism. Given the insights which a relevant course in the teaching of reading should aim to provide, the secondary specialist has opportunities to do much needed research into an area which has been almost completely neglected – teaching reading in the content fields. No one is better qualified than the subject specialist for this vital task. He is already an expert in the subject, in its technical vocabulary, in the concepts required and in the stages by which those concepts grow. He is also familiar with the diagrammatic and other nonverbal forms of reading related to his specialism. Also, if the readability of textbooks and technical literature is to be improved it is the subject specialist who has some expertise in teaching reading who alone will accomplish this effectively.

The secondary subject specialist of the future has an important part to play in the teaching of reading. It is a role for which he will be unfit and one which he will not accept unless his training equips him for it and enables him to approach his task with confidence and skill.

The LEAs
If there is to be a drive for reading improvement the schools need much more effective help than they have been getting from the LEAS. The latter could pay much more than mere lip service to the cause of reading extension by making a once-for-all equipment grant to enable

schools to purchase the necessary laboratory materials, including pupils' record books, teachers' manuals and supporting library resources. They could make more generous provision for secondment of personnel to in-service courses in the teaching of reading. They could appoint specialist advisers in reading (at all levels, not merely remedial) to promote reading extension throughout the schools in their area. The impending reorganization of local government into fewer and larger units should make all these provisions financially possible.

The publishers
At the moment there is little material at extension level, other than the SRA *Reading Laboratories* and the Ward Lock Educational *Reading Workshops*, available to teachers in schools. There is great scope for publishers to produce a developmental range of new materials aimed at the specific subskills of critical reading and at certain stages to provide practice material on which the subskills could be integrated and consolidated.

The researchers
Reading suffers from being overresearched. The theory goes piling up, little of it is conclusive, and hardly any of it seems worthy of consideration by the practising teacher in school. It might be a good thing if all research into the theoretical aspects of reading were stopped for a period of say five years. During that period efforts could be concentrated on the practice of teaching reading, especially at extension level. Almost all the research into the practical problems of teaching reading is devoted to beginning or remedial reading.

There is also a need for new and better reading tests. At present the only tests with which the majority of teachers are familiar are word recognition tests. It is hard to say exactly what such tests do measure apart from reading age. It is difficult to make any but the most minimal diagnostic use of the results, while the reading behaviour demanded of the testees is far too limited for worthwhile observation. What is needed is a much wider sampling of reading behaviour which would enable teachers to rapidly identify strengths and weaknesses and in the case of the latter to bring to bear appropriate treatment or enrichment. Certainly we need tests which would examine children's ability to read critically and efficiently.

The teacher-training establishments
The colleges of education and university training departments need to give still greater priority to the teaching of reading in initial professional courses. Despite recent improvements, provision in the colleges is very unequal and in some is quite inadequate. Many capable and experienced tutors, known by me personally, labour in vain to get college time to mount adequate courses and to link them practically

to work with children. Academic considerations in some colleges still rule out the provision of relevant and practical courses organized with the needs of schools in mind. Too many colleges are still only concerned with beginning reading. There is a great need to go beyond this and to initiate work at extension level, especially for the junior/ secondary student. The reading element in the professional training of postgraduate students is woefully inadequate. There is just not the time to integrate theory and practice in general crash courses of one year. Most of all there is a need to establish in some of our universities a chair in Reading. Only then will reading have the academic status needed to get off the ground at main subject level a new option in some colleges – a three-year course in the teaching of reading.

There remains one important area – the in-service field – which merits increased attention from the colleges. There are only four full-time in-service courses in the teaching of reading in England at the present time. Those at Edge Hill and Sheffield are one-year courses of advanced study leading to a Diploma in the Teaching of Reading. Mather College runs a one-term course each spring term in language arts in the primary and middle school with the teaching of reading as the major element and integrating factor. The one-term course at Reading has been specifically for college of education lecturers. All the courses mentioned attract many more would-be entrants than can be accepted. Unfortunately, the enthusiasm of the applicants is not matched by a general willingness on the part of LEAs to second them for the required periods. However, the fact that the courses are initially heavily oversubscribed is an indication that more are needed. That this occurs at a time when the peak of demand for preservice college places is past and some decline in student numbers is anticipated should give colleges good reason to expand their activities into the field of in-service training.

However, not all teachers necessarily want advanced diplomas, nor are many able for various reasons to attend full-time for as long as a term to a year, especially when this involves travelling difficulties or a temporary change of residence. There is a need to extend considerably the provision of short-term courses in specific areas of reading development and particularly for day-release facilities organized on a large scale by joint endeavours of LEAs and the colleges. Day-release obviates the problems of expense and teacher replacement associated with long periods of secondment. Teachers can be replaced for odd days by college students in functional teaching practice situations to the mutual advantage of both schools and colleges. The courses provided can have immediate relevance to the needs of local schools and could do much towards ending the separatism that characterizes much college, as opposed to school, activity.

The training of reading specialists
Those who train teachers have to cater for two sets of needs: the

needs of the students as individuals and the needs of the schools which those individuals will ultimately serve. Teacher training is judged by the success with which it satisfies the demands of the schools for better professional training and also by the degree to which it satisfies students that the courses are relevant for them personally, both as students in the short-term process of higher education and as people adequately trained to earn their living in the profession for which they have been trained. With increasing sensitivity to the needs of the schools, a number of area training organizations now include the teaching of reading as a compulsory element in the training of all teachers.

With these considerations in mind, it seems pertinent to enquire whether somewhat improved compulsory courses (at a very minimal level in many colleges) for all teachers are sufficient to satisfy society's demands for dramatically improved reading standards in the schools. Also, what of the students whose special qualities, abilities and interests incline them towards specializing in reading rather than in other fields? Will they be satisfied with the mere basic elements of a common college course?

Many colleges have recently adopted Third Area patterns of course organization. This means in practice that for the certificate students work in two areas, namely main subject and education, continues as in the past, but that the time formerly devoted to work at subsidiary level has now been allocated to a combination of optional and compulsory courses which can be seen to be more professionally relevant than those which they have replaced. It is due to the change to Third Area that many colleges now have the time to make the teaching of reading a compulsory requirement. However, with the advent of Third Area a set of conditions is emerging which appears favourable for meeting the needs of the schools and the preferences of a proportion of students for a broader and more detailed training in teaching reading than that given to the majority. There are two ways in which this might be achieved: first, by allowing a student who is so motivated to choose a range of options within the Third Area field associated with reading; alternatively, the teaching of reading could be elevated to main subject status leaving the optional field free for the development of other interests. Either mode would result in the training of a cadre of embryo reading specialists who, after some time in schools and possibly advanced study to follow, would achieve full professional specialist status. With reading difficulty a major problem at all levels of schooling and reading extension virtually uncharted territory, this is a development which the schools would welcome. Students so trained and whose testimonials and certificates were endorsed to indicate a major interest and qualification in the teaching of reading would certainly have no difficulty in finding work and could anticipate future opportunities for advancement in school and also in remedial, advisory and administrative capacities that compare

I

favourably with the career prospects of general practitioners.

There are many academic staff (all specialists in their own fields) in colleges and universities who object to specialized training in the teaching of reading. This is an odd view in that students in training already follow specialized courses for a large part of their time in college. They are generally divided into separate infant, or junior/ middle, or secondary groups, and the course work of each group has its own specialist orientation. On the academic side a student special- izes in a main subject which he pursues in depth for three years. There is an increasing tendency for the specialist subject departments to do their own 'method' work and to seek greater autonomy in supervising and organizing teaching practice arrangements for their specialisms, i.e. a hyperspecialist trend.

The objection to the teaching of reading has traditionally been that it is not an academic discipline and therefore is unsuitable as a main subject. Yet physical education, woodwork, metalwork, outdoor pur- suits, drama, dance, domestic science and primary French are all main subjects. They have achieved this status not because they are academic disciplines *per se* but because schools need to provide these activities and personnel have to be trained to teach them. The activities mentioned are important in the present-day school curri- culum. Is reading less so? From the viewpoint of academic discipline it would be interesting to compare the number of master's degrees gained in the teaching of reading with those awarded for the main subjects listed. It would be of equal interest to compare the volume of international research in the teaching of reading with that associated with the subjects mentioned or indeed with almost any other subject taught at main level in the colleges.

Other paradoxes occur in any discussion of the academic nature of main subjects. A secondary student majoring in geography, history, mathematics, French, English, music, or indeed in any of the tradi- tional main subjects, has a more than merely academic interest in his specialism. He would generally aim to earn his living by teaching his subject and his department spends a great deal of time and expertise in training him to do it. Even primary students find a vocational interest in main subjects such as PE, dance, drama, primary French and divinity, and it would be an unusual school which did not encourage some specialization for staff with specific qualifications in these fields. Would a qualification in teaching reading be less useful? On the other hand, there are some main subjects, e.g. sociology, which have no apparent direct vocational utility as a teaching subject in any but the upper forms of secondary schools, yet they are studied in depth for three years by people training to teach infants. It is an odd commentary on the relevance of professional training that until recently in one college a department fourteen strong taught students sociology for three and, in some cases, four years. Over that period of time the secondary students there had three lectures on how to teach reading.

Certain changes in college organization would be needed to provide the range of courses required to train reading specialists. The following courses at least would be required:

1 A course in the psychology of reading.
2 A developmental course in the teaching of reading from infant to adult level.
3 An advanced course in reading at the students' own level.
4 A course in linguistics.
5 A course in children's literature – not merely collecting titles and anthologies but actually reading the books, using speed reading techniques, and assessing them for readability for given age groups.
6 A course in librarianship.
7 Practical teaching exercises at three levels:
i To work through a particular programme drawn up by consultation between student, class teacher and reading tutor, the object being to expose the student to a sequence of experiences which become progressively more complex. For example, a student could begin by teaching an individual child, then a group of two or three, with growing confidence could extend the group to eight or ten, and in time could take over the reading needs of an entire class.
ii To teach two or three individual pupils over a period of the three years of the college course and to fully document the experience in detailed longitudinal case studies. The object would be for the student to be actively engaged in in-depth teaching and thus acquire insights into reading as a developmental process.
iii To be involved in the practical organization of reading development. For example, a group of third year students under their reading tutor could take over the reading needs of an entire school for one school term.

There are two ways in which the courses suggested could be provided. First, by setting up separate departments for the teaching of reading. The staff could be provided either by transfer from education departments which would cease to have responsibility for reading, and could therefore have their staffing ratios reduced proportionately, or by the appointment of specialist reading staff to replace tutors formerly supplying subsidiary courses which would be discontinued under Third Area arrangements. Either way there need be no overall increase in staffing to implement this policy.

Alternatively, the teaching of reading could be elevated to main subject level within the existing organizational framework by retaining responsibility for reading under the aegis of education departments. The latter are indeed generally well placed to effect such an extension of their traditional role. Usually they already have control over present reading policy and staff with interests and expertise in the field. They also have staff whose collective experience as practitioners usually covers the whole spectrum of formal education from preschool to university. Among them are usually to be found those with specialist qualifications in psychology, sociology, child development, curriculum development and educational technology, all of whom could make significant contributions to a main course in the teaching of reading. Education departments also administer teaching practice arrangements and could therefore assist in the organization of the clinical and longitudinal teaching exercises suggested. Courses in librarianship and in linguistics and children's literature could be organized on an interdepartmental basis by corporate endeavours of the library, English and education department staffs.

Bibliography

HUTCHINSON, M. and YOUNG, C. (1962) *Educating the Intelligent* Harmondsworth: Penguin.

INGLIS, W. B. (1968) 'The professional preparation of teachers of reading' in M. M. Clark and S. Maxwell (eds) *Reading: Influences on Progress* Edinburgh: UKRA

MINISTRY OF EDUCATION (1959) *Primary Education: Suggestions for the Consideration of Teachers and Others concerned with the Work of Primary Schools* London: HMSO

MORRIS, J. M. (1966) *Standards and Progress in Reading* Slough: NFER

MOYLE, D. and MOYLE, L. (1971) *Modern Innovations in the Teaching of Reading* London: University of London Press

NUT (1958) *The Curriculum of the Junior School* London: Schoolmaster Publishing Company

ROBINSON, H. M. (1964) 'Developing critical readers' in R. G. Stauffer (ed) *Dimensions of Critical Reading* Newark, Delaware: IRA

RUSSELL, D. H. (1964) *Children Learn to Read* Boston: Ginn

STOTT, D. H. (1962) *Programmed Reading Kit* Edinburgh: Holmes McDougall

TANSLEY, A. E. (1967) *Reading and Remedial Reading* London: Routledge and Kegan Paul

Index